BUILDING THE WEST RIDING

BUILDING THE WEST RIDING

A Guide to its Architecture and History

Lynn F Pearson

Smith Settle

First published in 1994 by
Smith Settle Ltd
Ilkley Road
Otley
West Yorkshire
LS21 3JP

ISBN   Paperback   1 85825 012 9
        Hardback   1 85825 013 7

British Library Cataloguing-in-Publication data:
A catalogue record for this book is available from the British Library.

Half-title page: Victoria Mill, Shipley.
Title page: Undercliffe Cemetery, Bradford.

Designed, printed and bound by
SMITH SETTLE
Ilkley Road, Otley, West Yorkshire LS21 3JP

Contents

Preface

Why does it look like that? An answer to this most basic question, whether applied to building or landscape, town or tunnel, takes in a whole complex of factors - finance, topography, politics and fashion, to name only four - which help determine what we see before us. This book is intended for travellers, whether on wheels, feet or of the armchair variety, who wish to know more about the history of the West Riding and its architecture, and the influences which have shaped the façades.

The West Riding has many attributes, one of which is sheer size. Buildings and structures from cathedrals to canals and monoliths to monuments fall within the grasp of this book, so the selection is necessarily personal but, I hope, comprehensive enough to satisfy and stimulate, and to act as an introduction to the architectural history of the area. I have suggested routes for walkers and drivers, and included several good viewpoints where the landscape lies before you, and often history begins to make more sense.

I make no apology for choosing to write about the Ridings rather than the more modern administrative counties of Yorkshire, nor for retaining miles and feet at the expense of kilometres and centimetres. Administrative boundaries can and do change over time, but the geographical limits of the Ridings are permanent, at least on the human timescale, and are more relevant to the architectural history of the area than current boundaries. In addition, the majority of the buildings described here were constructed using the traditional system of measurement.

So, where to begin? Such is the choice in the West Riding that any journey is likely to result in surprising discoveries. I have chosen seven personal favourites, the best of the West, or perhaps the seven wonders of the West Riding. This is not a choice based purely on architectural merit, or one designed to be representative of the totality of buildings in the Riding, but simply a selection of sites which have remained in my memory long after the first awe-inspiring glimpse.

Top of my list has to be the Studley Royal estate, with buildings ranging from Fountains Abbey through a seventeenth century prodigy house to the gloriously colourful Victorian church of St Mary.

Then, in no particular order, come the delicate iron and glass structure of Brook Street Market in Huddersfield, the Wainhouse Tower which looks south over the Calder Valley from Halifax, the Victorian Gothic towers of Allerton Park, the Dark Arches which support Leeds railway station, the beautiful and tranquil gardens of Parcevall Hall and finally the Garden Gate public house, Hunslet's magical Edwardian drinking palace. The railway viaducts, from the great Batty Moss at Ribblehead to those handsome but lesser-known specimens which enrich obscure corners of the West Riding, are also a special favourite of mine, as is the church of St John the Evangelist in Leeds.

The question of access to land and properties is often difficult. Footpaths are diverted and sometimes disappear altogether, as occasionally do buildings. However, opening hours for National Trust properties mentioned in the text (Fountains Abbey and Studley Royal, East Riddlesden Hall and Nostell Priory) and those in the care of English Heritage (Brodsworth Hall, Conisbrough Castle, Monk Bretton Priory, Roche Abbey, Aldborough Roman Town, Spofforth Castle and Studley Royal St Mary's Church) are available in the respective handbooks.

Other properties may open regularly, infrequently or not at all. I have described a few buildings which are not open to the public as I felt these to be of such importance in the history of the West Riding, so please respect the privacy of the owners. It is good to see so many properties opening under the aegis of the National Gardens and other similar schemes, often with the magic word 'Teas' following the garden description!

Buildings can make you gasp with surprise, puzzle you completely or even leave you cold. Whatever your reaction, there is nothing to beat seeing for yourself, and I hope this book will help you explore the West Riding and the best of its buildings, and explain just how and why they came to be as they are today.

When a book encompasses an area as vast as the West Riding, it is not surprising that the author's debts to individuals and organisations are equally great. I should particularly like to thank Rose Hill and Steve Jenkinson for their sterling hospitality, and Steve's response to a small query, which was almost a book in itself; Jim and Margaret Perry for heroic services to dog-sitting; David and Caroline da Costa for exploring the outer reaches of Sheffield; Trevor Ermel, who managed to produce prints even from a film which was run over; James Wyld for his advice on Todmorden; and the Riverdale House Country Hotel in Bainbridge, who rescued an errant film. This is not to forget Sue Hudson, Boots and Benson (and the late Sam), whose company was much appreciated. All errors and omissions are, of course, my own.

For their advice on the text, I should like to thank the following: the City Planning Officer at Bradford Metropolitan Council, Department of Planning at Craven District Council, Directorate of Planning at Doncaster Metropolitan Borough Council, Department of

Technical Services at Harrogate Borough Council, Economic Development and Planning Service at Kirklees Metropolitan Council, Chief Planning Officer at Leeds City Council, Development Department at Ribble Valley Borough Council, Department of Planning at Rotherham Metropolitan Borough Council, Department of Environmental Services at Selby District Council, Department of Land and Planning at Sheffield City Council, Planning Department at Wakefield Metropolitan District Council and the Yorkshire Dales National Park.

I am also grateful to the Bagshaw Museum, Bradford Industrial and Horses at Work Museum, British Waterways, Margaret Connor, Craven Museum, Hugh T Fattorini, Nidderdale Museum Society and the North Craven Building Preservation Trust Limited for their assistance in the preparation of this book.

I am grateful to the following for their courtesy in granting permission to reproduce illustrations: Bradford Heritage Recording Unit, City Engineer of Bradford Metropolitan Council, Bramham Park, Board of Trustees of Carlton Towers, Peter Cook, Courage Limited, FaulknerBrowns, Moravian Museum at Fulneck, Halifax Building Society, Museum of North Craven Life, Newby Hall and Gardens, Nidderdale Museum, Julie Phipps and Skipton Castle.

Trevor Mitchell provided the line drawings which grace the text; Richard Littlewod took the photograph of the Garden Gate public house. All other illustrations are the author's own.

Lynn F Pearson
Gosforth, Newcastle upon Tyne
1994

Acknowledgments

The publishers and author would like to thank the following for permission to reproduce the illustrations listed below:

Bradford Heritage Recording Unit, p99; Bramham Park, pp10, 11; Board of Trustees, Carlton Towers, pp148, 149; Courage Limited, p151; FaulknerBrowns, p170 (Julie Phipps), p193 (Peter Cook); Halifax Building Society, pp131, 133; J R Knight, City Engineer, Bradford Metropolitan Council, p96; Richard Littlewood, p75; Moravian Museum, Fulneck, pp84, 85; Museum of North Craven Life, p60; Newby Hall & Gardens, pp21, 22, 23; Nidderdale Museum, p33; Skipton Castle, pp54, 55.

The line drawings are by Trevor Mitchell.

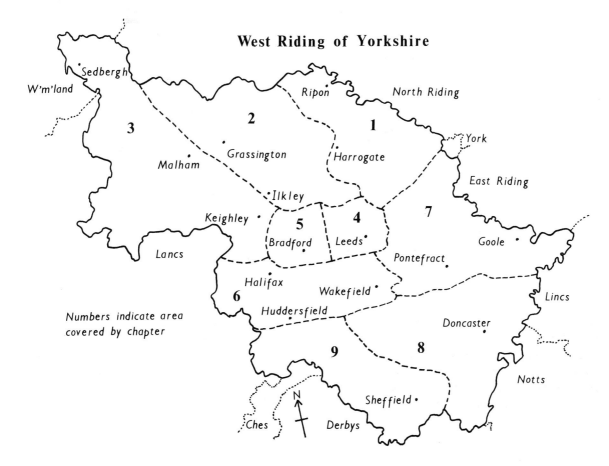

West Riding of Yorkshire

Numbers indicate area covered by chapter

FROM CRIMPLE TO CRYPT

Harrogate and the North-East

To see Harrogate as a whole - impossible from within the steep valley setting of the town itself - follow the path which runs west through Valley Gardens from the centre of Harrogate. After just over a mile of gentle ascent it reaches Harlow Hill, on the edge of the moors. Here, from beside an elegant water tower and a strange observatory, an impressive view opens out east over Harrogate, revealing the lie of the land and buildings old and new.

The settlement of Harrogate was established by the early 1300s and grew in a long, straggling pattern with today's High Harrogate at its south-eastern end. Low Harrogate, on the site of the present town centre, expanded in the sixteenth or seventeenth century, but Harrogate's eventual fame and fortune rested on the presence of mineral water springs. William Slingsby, uncle of the Knaresborough MP of the same name, realised in 1571 that the waters of the Tewit Well resembled those of the Belgian resort of Spa. The nearby Sweet Spaw was discovered in 1631, and a total of eighty-eight springs within a two mile radius meant that spring water was never in short supply.

Visitors were attracted to take the waters, and the first major hotel was built around 1687. Hotel development was concentrated on High Harrogate, though visitors had also discovered the Sulphur Well at Low Harrogate. Due to the severe northern weather, social life in Harrogate, in contrast to the sunnier southern spas, was based on the hotels as lack of capital investment precluded the construction of assembly rooms and the like.

By the mid-eighteenth century, Harrogate was an established and prosperous spa town, but this happy situation was threatened in the 1760s by the possibility of enclosure of land around the mineral springs. Pressure on Parliament resulted in the 1778 Award to the town of the Stray, 200 acres of common land which included all the known springs. Harrogate's continuing popularity with the aristocracy was ensured by the erection of a theatre in 1788 and the opening of a racecourse on the Stray in 1793. Nearly 2,500 visitors came to Harrogate in 1795, this total excluding their servants.

The start of the nineteenth century saw Harrogate aspiring to be a full-blown resort, but lacking the necessary amenities. The townspeople began to remedy this by subscribing to build an assembly room in 1804. It opened two years later and was followed by the Victoria and Montpellier Baths and the Classical Spa Rooms in the 1830s. The arrival of the railway in 1848 heralded change, in the social class of Harrogate's visitors and eventually in the pattern of entertainment buildings, as the fruits of Northern industrialisation began to provide funds for capital investment. By the town's Edwardian heyday, taking the waters was complemented by less stringent pleasures.

Before leaving Harlow Hill to explore the town, take a closer look at the pair of towers which stand beside the path. The gloriously Classical water tower of 1902 was built by Harrogate Corporation waterworks engineer Edward Wilson Dixon, who piled up the Classical motifs on a rusticated octagonal sandstone base. The circular windowed tower is adorned with pilasters, and topping it all an ironwork honeysuckle motif runs around the rim of the water tank. Its neighbour is the ninety foot high Harlow Hill Tower, built in 1829 by John Thompson for use as an observatory and opened to the public, at a charge of sixpence, by 1900. It is a severely plain tower of square cross-section.

Leaving the towers and Harlow Moor behind, the Royal Pump Room is less than a mile away, down through weird Bogs Field and the almost sub-tropical Valley Gardens.

Bogs Field acquired its name from the mineral springs rising to its surface; unusually, these do not contain meteoric water, originating in rainfall, but magmatic water produced by a cooling igneous rock mass below the earth's surface.

Valley Gardens, replete with wells, leads on to the Classical Royal Pump Room of 1842 with its 1913 glazed addition, the combination now a museum. The domed octagonal Pump Room was built to house the Old Sulphur Well; it was designed by local man Isaac Thomas Shutt and built of local sandstone. Its extension, in iron and glass winter garden style, was needed to accommodate the numbers of people visiting Harrogate to take the waters in the early years of the twentieth century, when the town was known as the 'World's Greatest Spa'.

Along Crescent Road lies the unexciting grey stone façade of the Royal Baths, enlivened only by twin towers and a dome. This hydrotherapy centre opened in 1897 and housed a vast range of bathing and treatment rooms originally decorated with a fabulous array of marbles, mosaics, and ornate wood and plasterwork. The Royal Baths was designed by London architects Frank Baggallay and F E Bristowe. The west wing extension was opened in 1939. The building as a whole is typical of much Harrogate architecture in that a sober, grey façade hides a spectacular interior.

The Royal Baths faces its royal partner, the Kursaal or Royal Hall, across the busy Kings Road junction. The delightfully eclectic exterior of the Royal Hall, topped by a lantern which would look more at home on the end of a pier, has been marred only by the addition of an awful canopy on its Ripon Road façade. But do not let this excrescence deter you from viewing the interior, often open for concerts and exhibitions. The Royal Hall was designed by J R Beale, and was originally intended to be a pleasure centre based on a 3,000 seat hall with ancilliary billiard rooms, restaurants and other facilities. Local councillors vetoed this ambitious plan, and the 1,200 capacity Royal Hall opened in 1903. The interior, a flat-floored theatre, was by Frank Matcham, Britain's premier theatre designer, and is one of his most opulent works, crowned by a splendid ceiling.

Beside the Royal Hall a footpath leads away from Ripon Road up to the terrace garden of the Majestic Hotel, a fine spot for surveying Harrogate's equally majestic collection of hotels. The Majestic itself was something of a latecomer, opening in 1900; the Crown, with its idiosyncratic tower, and the Old Swan date from the eighteenth century and many more were erected during the nineteenth century. The Majestic was designed by G D Martin, a London-based architect specialising in offices and hotels. Its red brick now complements the bright, confident red and white of the circular central bastion of the Conference Centre, which opened in 1981.

The bulk of the Conference Centre and its hotel partner are most visible from the northern approaches to Harrogate, standing out on the skyline like a medieval castle. Other new development, particularly on Parliament Street alongside the Royal Baths, is of a lesser quality. The highlight of Parliament Street is the Germano-Gothic Westminster Arcade of 1898, all turrets and towers, and at the top of the street is a glimpse

A concert at the winter gardens in the early twentieth century.

of what might be termed 'Harrogate Baronial' on the curve of Cornwall Road. Also on Cornwall Road, look out for some fine leaded glass with swan motifs at first floor level on the Sothebys building.

Just off Parliament Street in narrow Oxford Street are two massive façades: the Wesley Chapel, built by Lockwood and Mawson of Bradford in 1862; and the Harrogate Theatre, built as the Grand Opera House in 1900 by architect John P Briggs. Briggs, once Frank Matcham's clerk of works, designed thirteen theatres between 1897 and 1908. His Opera House exterior is in Arts and Crafts style, complete with an octagonal four-storey tower, but the intimate interior is richly decorated with typical late Victorian enthusiasm.

Yet more pleasure buildings enliven the townscape. From Parliament Street, past the elegant interiors of James Street and over the almost invisible railway, in Station Avenue lies the Odeon. It was opened in September 1936 and designed by Harry Weedon (1888-1970), consultant architect to the Odeon Theatre chain owned by Oscar Deutsch. During the late 1930s Weedon brought Odeon building to the height of perfection, reducing construction time to seven or eight months for the smaller cinemas and standardising the house style. The Harrogate Odeon's green, red and white ceramic tile façade with its central tower is typical of Weedon's designs. The cinema is now a listed building and happily still fulfils its original function.

The North Eastern public house, back over the railway on the corner of Albert Street, also continues to serve its clientele in the surrounds of an excellent display of Edwardian joinery. Continuing up Station Parade to the Stray, the close-knit buildings open out on to the common, where the visitor will find a minor Tuscan temple. This is the Tewit Well, the original source of water and wealth for the Queen of Inland Watering Places.

The railway has little public presence in Harrogate largely because of early fears that the view across the Stray, Harrogate's common, would be ruined by the intrusion of trains and track. A terminus opened on the 20th July 1848 and a through station was finally completed in 1862, the tracks cutting across the town below street level. By this means the Stray was preserved apparently intact. The almost complete demolition of the through station in 1964 and the erection of a vile façade have contrived to hide the existence of Harrogate's railway altogether.

Fortunately, more fitting reminders of the railway age lie to the south and east of Harrogate. In the peaceful valley of Crimple Beck, two miles south of the town near the village of Pannal, stands a monument to the engineers of the Victorian railway. The thirty-one buff sandstone arches of the mighty Crimple Viaduct, designed by John C Birkinshaw for the York & North Midland Railway in 1848, cross the beck 110 feet below. Each arch spans fifty feet and the whole structure stretches for 624 yards. The viaduct formed a vital part of the Harrogate-Church Fenton railway line; trains out of Harrogate then ran east from the viaduct, towards Wetherby, but now head west via a steep connection to the line which originally continued under its arches. This was owned by the Leeds & Thirsk Railway, and ran through the eastern fringe of Harrogate, stopping at Starbeck.

The happy conjunction of railway and beck made construction of the viaduct essential; although by no means Yorkshire's tallest or longest, Crimple Viaduct is a particularly elegant specimen. The peace of the valley it crosses is only disturbed by the screeching of train wheels attempting to round the curving approach from Pannal Station. The viaduct looms in the distance ahead of drivers heading

Crimple Viaduct, Pannal, near Harrogate.

north on the A61 from Pannal to Harrogate, but for a closer view take the path beside the beck. A footpath meanders from Pannal churchyard eastwards out of the village; this is part of the Harrogate Ringway, which encircles the town. It eventually forks, one path heading towards the southern suburbs of Harrogate and the other passing under the viaduct.

Pannal itself, burned by the Scots in a 1318 post-Bannockburn raid, is now a commuter village, a stone-built outlier of Harrogate. Before Harrogate opened its own workhouse in 1810, the town paid to house its paupers in Pannal Workhouse. Pannal Church, dedicated to St Robert of Knaresborough, is home to a beautiful grey-white Italian marble font, said to have come from Fountains Abbey in the seventeenth century. Whatever the provenance, its oval shape and smooth curves render it a lovely and most unusual object.

To the east of Harrogate the railway continues to Knaresborough, or the walker can follow the Nidd Gorge Nature Trail; this starts on the northern edge of Harrogate at Bilton Lane and passes the now-disused Nidd railway viaduct before ending just west of Knaresborough.

The spectacular castellated Knaresborough Viaduct dominates the centre of the town, bridging the Nidd Gorge in four great leaps. The first railway viaduct on the site, intended to be part of the line connecting York and Harrogate, collapsed in 1848 when on the point of completion. It was immediately rebuilt by railway engineer Thomas Grainger, and opened in 1851. Grainger was a Scottish civil engineer and surveyor who moved into railway work in the 1820s and never looked

back, his practice extending throughout Scotland and as far south as Yorkshire.

It is impossible to avoid using the term picturesque when describing Knaresborough, its buildings tumbling around the dramatic sandstone cliffs of the Nidd Gorge, with the whole topped by the ruins of a fourteenth century castle. Knaresborough Castle is now no more than a keep, gatehouse and the remains of a towered curtain wall, but it was once a royal castle of some importance, its walls reaching forty feet in height. Historically, Knaresborough was a more important and larger town than Harrogate; the Royal Forest of Knaresborough was in existence in the early twelfth century, and the fourteenth century court house of the Forest Court of Knaresborough survives in the castle's outer bailey. In 1664 hearth tax returns showed Knaresborough to have 156 houses compared with Harrogate's 57, but now the small market town has been left behind by the resort in terms of population.

The site of the castle provides a fine viewpoint over town and gorge. Close to the castle is Market Place, with its Classical town hall (1862), and the route down to the riverside along Kirkgate to Waterside leads through much pleasant Georgian domestic building. It is Waterside's continuation Abbey Road, however, which yields a most peculiar pair of structures.

The Chapel of Our Lady of the Crag is a tiny shrine carved out of the side of the cliff. The shrine was founded in 1409, and is guarded by the larger-than-life size armoured figure of a knight holding a sword. Above the cave is another oddity, Fort Montagu, a house dating from 1770 cut into the rockface. It took sixteen years for a weaver and his son to excavate their castellated abode, its name taken from the weaver's patron, Lady Elizabeth Montagu.

The railway continues eastward from Knaresborough, down the magnesian limestone ridge and into the Ouse basin, passing through Kirk Hammerton before crossing the meandering Nidd and heading for York. St John the Baptist at Kirk Hammerton is an almost complete Saxon church of around 1050, albeit with extensions and a restoration in 1891 by Charles Hodgson Fowler. From the south, most of the modern work is hidden and the power of the hefty blocks of rough-hewn Saxon masonry can easily be seen. The north wall was removed about 1200 to make way for another aisle, but the chancel arch is mainly Saxon work.

Three miles north-east of Kirk Hammerton along Pool Lane lies Nun Monkton, where a Benedictine nunnery was founded around 1150. Nothing survives of the home of the prioress and her twelve nuns except the nave of the church of St Mary, built around 1180, though the fine west front may date from 1230-40. The aisleless nave is lit by arcades made up of lancet windows, similar to the clerestories of a cathedral. The present east end was added in the 1873 restoration, and contains three lancet windows with stained glass by William Morris & Company; this is some of the finest stained glass in the West Riding. Nun Monkton Hall, south of the church, was built around 1690 in stone, using the Classical style with an unusual façade of giant pilasters. The hall's garden reaches down to the banks of the Ouse, the boundary between West and East Ridings.

Travelling southwards from Knaresborough, five miles along the B6163 and A661, we find Spofforth, a village with buildings spanning medieval to Victorian times. The ruin of Spofforth Castle, a fortified manor house, lies on the western edge of the village. Licence to crenellate was granted in 1308 to Henry Percy; the village was one of the main seats of the Percy family and important for their iron industry until Alnwick in Northumberland was acquired in the fourteenth century. Henry Percy built his house directly against the rockface, and remains of the great hall, solar and kitchen, with its two large fireplaces, are visible, as are a few fragments of other buildings, showing that the house was part of a quadrangle. The castle was wrecked by Sir Henry Percy's enemies after his death at the battle of Towton, just south of Tadcaster, in 1461. Further demolition followed in 1650. The village church, All Saints, appears to be a Norman Revival model, but the 1855 exterior hides real Norman work within, including beakhead and zigzag decoration.

Just east of the church, a path leads north beside Crimple Beck to cross the A661 two miles farther on near Plumpton Hall, actually a stable block converted to living quarters for Daniel Lascelles soon after 1760. Daniel's brother Edwin Lascelles inherited the nearby Harewood estate in 1753 and built Harewood House, taking much interest in the design. Daniel had less grand ambitions, although he did begin to build a mansion on the Plumpton site, but it was never finished.

Opposite Plumpton, across Crimple Beck, lies Rudding Park, an otherwise severe Classical house happily adorned with five bow windows. The architect was Robert Chantrell, a pupil of Sir John Soane, who moved to Leeds in 1819 and built up a practice as a specialist in Gothic churches. Rudding Park was begun in 1805 by an unknown architect, Chantrell taking over and completing the work after 1824. The ornate private chapel (1874) is the size of a small church.

Three miles east of Plumpton by footpath is Little Ribston and the Ribston Hall estate, reached from the village via a footpath which crosses the Nidd. The hall, stretching to fifteen bays in brick, was built for Sir Henry Goodricke in 1674. The red-brick stables were added around 1775, probably by John Carr, who may also have designed the Gothick arch in the park.

From Spofforth, the road to Wetherby passes Stockeld Park, a heavily impressive James Paine creation of 1758-63 built for William Middleton. The owner's death, caused by gout, made completion of further estate improvements impossible, but Paine remarked that no expense was spared on the house in order to make it 'permanent and beautiful'. Although much of the interior has been altered, the dramatic domed elliptical staircase hall remains. The nearby chapel was enlarged in 1909 by Detmar Blow, the Arts and Crafts architect who had been inspired in his early years by working with John Ruskin.

East of Stockeld, a footpath runs across the main road and the abandoned Harrogate-Church Fenton railway line to the village of Kirk Deighton and its church, All Saints. The church retains a Norman north doorway and arcade, with fourteenth century work on the south and in the tower. The restoration of 1875 left All Saints with its most memorable

element, the richly-coloured Minton tiles framing the altar.

Wetherby, on the north bank of the River Wharfe, is often remembered only for its racecourse and bypass, and recently the use of its name as a film title, rather than for any intrinsic merits it might posess. This anonymity hides a town mentioned in the *Domesday* survey and connected with the Percy family from 1086, when the Norman lord William de Percy held part of the manor of Wetherby. By the early twelfth century, when Wetherby Castle was constructed, the Percy estates in Yorkshire included Spofforth, Tadcaster and Wetherby, and the family also held land in Lincolnshire.

Wetherby's progress towards the status of market town was helped by the building of a bridge over the Wharfe in the early thirteenth century; previously the only crossing had been a ford. In 1240, local landowners the Knights Templar were granted a royal charter for a weekly market in the town, and by the end of the century the road through Wetherby was an important part of the route linking England and Scotland. Wetherby continued its growth as a market town for the surrounding area into the late seventeenth century, by which time it had become an administrative centre and a meeting place for local communities, and had acquired a social structure distinctly different from that of its rural hinterland. The manor had also become the property of the Cavendish family, later Dukes of Devonshire, coming into their hands in the early seventeenth century.

On the 11th March 1723 the Great Fire of Wetherby, which began in a chandler's shop where tallow boiled over, destroyed more than half the properties in the town; many residents took out insurance policies in the months following the fire. Depression hit the farming industry of the Vale of York during the 1730s and 1740s, and, combined with the after-effects of the fire, caused the town's prosperity to decline. Towards the end of the century, when Harrogate and Boston were growing towns, Wetherby stagnated; its residents, unsupported by their absentee landlords the Devonshires, lacked the influence to change the course of events.

By the early years of the nineteenth century the Devonshire landholding comprised nine-tenths of Wetherby. Soon after inheriting the Devonshire estates the young sixth duke was forced to sell some of his property, in order to satisfy his extravagant architectural (and other) tastes. Wetherby, by then not a particularly profitable holding, was sold by auction at the Great Sale in October 1824. Though many residents bought their own homes, most of the land was purchased by outsiders; the sale raised £168,561. During the 1830s Wetherby was still an important staging point for coaches, and the arrival of the railway in 1847 did little to affect this trade until the 1860s. By then the steeplechases at the Linton Ings riverside course, laid out in 1842-3 to the south of the town, had become a great attraction. Racing began at the present course, York Road, in 1891.

Victorian and early twentieth century development didnot impinge much upon the little market town. The buildings of Wetherby (population just under 10,000 in 1981) reflect its status as a town bypassed not only by the Great North Road (in 1959) but by great historical events. Its finest buildings are two coaching inns, the Angel, and the Swan and Talbot, both dating from the early eighteenth century. Wetherby Bridge, two of its six arches being of medieval work, is a listed structure but lacks the monumentality that might be expected on the road to the north.

The Wharfe is bridged upstream at Linton, the road leading on to Collingham and the possibility of a journey west along the ridge-top road to Harewood House. The road, in part an elegant wooded avenue, gives good views to the north over the Wharfe Valley, incipient Wharfedale. Two miles further down the Leeds road is Bardsey, where All Hallows Church boasts a Saxon tower and Norman internal decorative work; north of the church is the mound or motte on which Bardsey Castle once stood. The tiny tenth century church, its nave only thirty-one feet long, expanded first with the addition of a north aisle in 1100-25, then a south aisle around fifty years later. It was again enlarged in the thirteenth century, with more alterations in the fifteenth century and a restoration in 1909. Thus did the fabric of the church cater for the growth of the congregation.

About four miles due east of Bardsey, almost along the line of a Roman road, lies Bramham. The chancel of battlemented All Saints Church, in the centre of the village, is lined with Art Nouveau panelling, an unusual addition dating from just before the First World War. The Bramham Park estate is on the far side of the A1, the house a product of the great Yorkshire tradition of amateur architects, particularly strong in the eighteenth century. The Bramham estate was inherited by Robert Benson, who became the first Lord Bingley in 1713. Benson travelled abroad in

Trimming the beech hedges at Bramham Park in the early twentieth century.

the last years of the seventeenth century, and on his return entered public life, rapidly advancing to become Chancellor of the Exchequer in 1711.

It seems that Benson was his own architect, probably building Bramham Park between 1699 and 1710. He also advised landowning friends on improvements to their houses. For his own home Benson produced a severely plain design in buff sandstone, three storeys high and eleven bays long. A fire in 1828 destroyed most of the interior, though the Stone Hall, a thirty foot cube, survived minus its ceiling. Restoration of the interior did not take place until 1907.

The glory of Bramham Park is its grounds, a complex of cascades, canals and avenues tricked out with temples, all in the style of the French landscape gardener LeNotre, much admired by Benson. The high beech hedges were part of the original plan, shown on an engraving of the garden made around 1725

Five beech avenues meet at the Urn of the Four Faces in Bramham Park; an early twentieth century view.

The Anglican church of St Luke, Clifford.

by surveyor John Wood. Wood was employed at Bramham during 1722-7, contributing to the development of the gardens and in 1725 drawing up initial plans for the future layout of the city of Bath. The second Lord Bingley, George Fox Lane, inherited the Bramham estate in 1731 and added an eye-catching and confusing assortment of temples, obelisks and cascades. The gardens suffered terrible gale damage in February 1962 when 490 trees were destroyed, including the oldest, but replanting has since taken place.

The road north of Bramham village leads to Boston Spa via Clifford, where the mighty Romanesque church of St Edward, King and Confessor is to be found. Its tower dominates the low-lying village and its presence overshadows the Anglican church of St Luke, a pretty little work designed in 1841 by J B Atkinson of the York architectural dynasty.

The Roman Catholic church of St Edward was built in 1845-8 by Joseph Hansom of cab fame, though the original design was by a young Scottish artist called Ramsay who produced his idealised plan for a church in the French Romanesque style when abroad. Henry Constable-Maxwell of nearby Stockeld Park met Ramsey on a shooting trip to Scotland

and bought the plans. Mrs Grimston, wife of the owner of Clifford's flax mill, and the first priest, Father Clifford, were the driving forces behind the building of the church. Funds were raised by an itinerant priest who managed to solicit contributions from the Pope, the Queen of France, the Grand Duke of Parma, the King of Sardinia and many wealthy Yorkshire Catholics. Indeed, this must have been a hugely enjoyable fund-raising exercise. Four stained glass windows were designed by A W N Pugin in 1848-51, and the tower was added in 1859-67 by Sheffield architect George Goldie.

Any one of four small lanes will take the traveller north from Clifford to Boston Spa. The architecture of this fine, stone-built Georgian town has everything its larger

The tower of St Edward rising above the village of Clifford.

neighbour Wetherby seems to lack by way of substantial buildings and imposing façades. Use of the local creamy-white magnesian limestone has resulted in an elegant vista along High Street, which sadly also has the traffic problems Wetherby now avoids. The spring waters were discovered by labourer John Shires in 1744, on the south bank of the Wharfe opposite the village of Thorp Arch. Early visitors had to stay on the north bank and cross to the spring by ferry, but in 1853 an entrepreneurial local man by the name of Joseph Tate (or Taite) built a house known as the Black Bull near the spring; this was the beginning of the new settlement, Boston Spa. The Wharfe was bridged at Thorp Arch in 1770, and increased access brought more visitors. A pump room and bath house were in place by 1792. By 1822 Boston had 600 inhabitants, and the spa was a well-known resort by the 1830s. A century later the spa was still popular as an excursion destination. Out of sight to the north of Boston is the British Library, unbecomingly disguised as a warehouse on the Thorp Arch Trading Estate.

To the east of Boston Spa the land rolls gently down to the Ouse basin, an area littered with tiny villages and cut through by drainage dikes. At Healaugh, five miles east of Thorp Arch, is the Norman church of St John, perhaps built about 1130-50. Its south doorway is decorated with human figures as well as zigzag and beakhead patterns, and beasts roam amongst the foliage on the capital heads. Inside, more animals are to be found on the shafts of the chancel arch.

Two miles north of Healaugh is the village of Long Marston. The road leading out of the village towards Tockwith marks the dividing line between Parliamentarian and Royalist forces at the battle of Marston Moor, fought on the 2nd July 1644. An obelisk commemorating the site of the battle stands where Moor Lane meets the Tockwith road. It is a plain, unmemorable structure, hardly significant enough to mark the field where around 6,000 men died and the Royalist threat in the North was all but obliterated.

The road west from Tockwith meets the Great North Road after running alongside the meandering Nidd and passing through Cowthorpe.

The tower of the oddly-structured church of St Michael appears to be perched upon a massive arch formed from two buttresses. The church was built in 1456-68 and houses the Easter Sepulchre, a wooden chest covered by a canopy in Perpendicular style. This was intended to hold the sacrament and crucifix from Maundy Thursday or Good Friday until Easter.

The hamlet of Allerton Mauleverer, and its mansion Allerton Park, lie four miles to the north, the shining dome of a circular Classical temple alerting drivers on the Great North Road to the presence of one of the West Riding's finest Victorian houses. All that can be seen from the road is a tangle of turrets, the house being reached from a lane leading off the A59, past a lodge house with bargeboards curling in the local manner. The church of St Martin squats at the end of the lane, almost a small-scale translation of Hawksmoor from east London, but in fact a James Paine or John Vardy design of 1745. There is a fine hammerbeam roof, quite overpowering in the small nave, and a painting of Moses and Aaron above the chancel arch; painting, pews,

The church of St Martin, Allerton Mauleverer.

pulpit and benches were all part of the original design.

A house has existed at Allerton since the late 1780s, and the present Allerton Park is a combination of Victorian and earlier work. The overwhelming Gothic mansion revealed on entering the grounds was built for Charles, Lord Stourton, by architect G Martin. Demolition of parts of the old house began on the 4th September 1848 and building works continued until 1852, though because of lack of funds the whole of the plan was never implemented. Quite enough was completed to take the breath away on first sight of the exterior, as towers and turrets reach upwards above the central clerestory, all held to earth by a massive porch. The interior is a feast of wood panelling, crockets and finials, with a hammerbeam roof in the great hall. The Stourton family left the house in 1965, taking much of the original furnishings with them (though not the Thurston billiard table), but restoration since 1981 has resulted in a spectacular display of Gothic taste.

Four miles north-east along a path leading from the park gate through Allerton

The central clerestory is visible above the turrets of Allerton Park.

Allerton Park: the south front.

The lodge house at Allerton Park.

Mauleverer lies the village of Little Ouseburn, once the setting for Kirby Hall, about which arguments raged amongst some of the great names of Georgian architecture. Stephen Thompson, owner of Kirby Hall Park, consulted Colonel James Moyser about the design of his new home in 1746. Moyser, an amateur architect much involved with the designs for Bretton Hall and Nostell Priory in the 1730s, provided Thompson with a plan for the future Kirby Hall, and suggested London architect Roger Morris should be consulted. Thompson admired Moyser's plan, but altered it without the colonel's approval. Morris was persuaded to visit Kirby Hall in 1747 and drew up a new elevation with the help of Lord Burlington, amateur architect and promoter of the Palladian style.

*Holy Trinity, Little Ouseburn, and the
Thompson Mausoleum.*

London architect Robert Lugar, a specialist in Picturesque cottages. Kirby Hall Park was landscaped by prolific country house architect J B Papworth, who added a conservatory in 1833. The most tangible reminder of the Thompson family is their mausoleum, to be found competing for space with the church of Holy Trinity in its churchyard facing the park. The solid domed temple is also a memorial to Palladian taste, with its thirteen Tuscan columns. It was built for Henry Thompson in the late eighteenth century, although the church, in its beautiful rural setting, dates from the Norman period.

The road leading north-east from the church passes an ice house, soon after another Kirby Hall lodge, and continues to the shivering timbers of Aldwark Bridge over the Ure; this is the North Riding border. Just inside the West Riding is the toll house, for one must pay to cross the river, and a particularly elegant example of glazing in a triangular pattern on a house to the south.

The Roman road now known as the B6265 takes the traveller north towards Aldborough, or Isurium Brigantum, originally the camp of the Ninth Legion in the first century AD. It was sited at the junction of four main roads and the highest point of navigation on the Ure (the Ouse in its northern reaches), and by AD 150 it was an important township of the Brigantes, the north British hill tribe. The settlement was encircled by a red sandstone wall twenty foot high, some of which remains, but the greatest attractions of Isurium are two unique mosaic pavements which belonged to one of seven Roman town houses on the site. The mosaics still remain in their original positions, surrounded by the wonderfully

Thompson himself produced the plan, and employed the young John Carr, then a stonemason, to supervise the works and add internal details during 1747-55. The result was a fine piece of Palladian design, but all we can now admire are its surroundings, as Kirby Hall was demolished in 1920.

At the end of the village street is an early nineteenth century park lodge designed by

*One of the three Devil's Arrows
near Boroughbridge*

fruitful gardens of modern residents. The decline of Aldborough began with the bridging of the Ure at Boroughbridge in Norman times. By the end of the thirteenth century much of the road traffic between Scotland and the south passed through Boroughbridge, which profited from diverting the road through its market place.

By the mid-eighteenth century, increasing traffic on the Great North Road, including cattle driven to the London markets and 6,000 wagons laden with coal and lime each year, had caused the road to deteriorate in the Boroughbridge area to such a state that coach travellers had to make detours. A turnpike trust was formed to improve the road, and the town continued to prosper, its many inns serving road and river traffic. The market cross of 1875 dominates cobbled Market Square, but the town's most significant buildings are its inns, which mainly line the old Great North Road.

Dividing Boroughbridge from the A1 to the west is a line of standing stones, the Devil's Arrows. Legend has it that they were arrows fired by the Devil from How Hill, near Fountains Abbey, in an effort to destroy Christian Aldborough. The evil archer's aim was not true and the four arrows fell short; little surprise, as they each weigh thirty-six tons.

One arrow was pulled down in the sixteenth century, but the three which remain form a line nearly 200 yards long, easily visible from the A1. The tallest is twenty-two feet six inches high, and all are made from millstone grit quarried at Knaresborough. The grooves in the tops of the stones may be due to weathering, or perhaps were made in the course of their transportation and erection. The stones are probably the southernmost of the set of Neolithic and Bronze Age monuments or henges which extend north-west towards West Tanfield, near Ripon.

Roecliffe Lane leads west from Borough-bridge and passes close by the southernmost of the Devil's Arrows before reaching Roecliffe and its jolly Gothic school of 1875, overlooking the village green. The neo-Norman church of St Mary was built in 1843-4 by Richard Hey Sharp, and is roofed by a great limestone barrel-vault. The hefty buttresses on the north and south walls of the church were added when the vault was thought to be failing in the 1870s. The atmospheric interior, probably modelled on an Oxford college chapel, is lined by raised benches on north, south and west walls, with a lectern at the west end. The furnishings comprise a collection of unusual religious oddments, including an old vestry door from York Minster, a Jacobean pulpit and picturesque oak panelling on the vestry walls.

A footpath beside Roecliffe Church takes the walker down to the south bank of the Ure and along to Lock House; the Newby Hall estate lies a little further upstream on the north bank. The lock at Lock House allowed river traffic to enter a cut of the Ure Navigation to the north. Making the Ure navigable from its junction with the Swale upwards to Ripon involved improvement of the Ure and construction of the two mile Ripon Canal between Ox Close and Ripon; the work took place in 1767-72 and cost £16,400. The entire navigation was sold to the Leeds & Thirsk Railway in 1847, as the railway company hoped to obtain local support for their line by

The church of St Mary, Roecliffe.

means of the purchase, following which the canal went into a slow decline. The limit of navigation is now about a mile north of Ox Close, but the canal still exists in Ripon and should eventually be fully reopened.

A mile north of Lock House across the Ure is Skelton, but the nearest river crossing is back in Boroughbridge. In Skelton stands one

The stone barrel vault in Roecliffe Church.

of the two most exciting Victorian churches in the West Riding (or even England). Just inside the grounds of Newby Hall is the church of Christ the Consoler, built by arch-medievalist William Burges for Lady Mary Vyner in memory of her youngest son Frederick Grantham Vyner, who was killed by Greek bandits while visiting the battlefield of Marathon. The church was commissioned in 1870, begun the following year and consecrated in 1876; the cost was about £25,000. The relatively plain exterior belies the glowing richness within. It is replete with red, green and black marble, and stained glass, all designed by Burges to produce a decorative effect from his favourite thirteenth century. Burges also designed St Mary's at Studley Royal in the same style for Frederick Grantham's brother-in-law, the pair of churches, less than seven miles apart, forming a neo-medieval masterpiece. Apart from an unbuilt design for Bradford Exchange (1863-4), these two churches are the only major works by Burges in the whole of Yorkshire.

A solid, rusticated line of lodges and gates marks the Skelton entrance to Newby Hall. One lodge has bulbous ball finials, and the whole array was designed by Yorkshireman William Belwood around 1780. Belwood was trained by Robert Adam, and supervised construction work at Harewood House in the 1760s before setting up on his own account at York in 1774. In 1780 his design was chosen ahead of John Carr's for the Newby Hall stables.

The hall itself was financed by the coalmining fortune of the Blacketts of Newcastle and Wallington. It was erected in the early 1690s for Sir Edward Blackett, but much was added in 1767-80 by the immensely fashionable Robert Adam. The hall was then owned by rich antique collector William Weddell, recently returned from his Grand Tour and with many new purchases to accommodate. Newby's red-brick exterior is impressive, but the best lies within: the Adam sculpture galleries.

The most spectacular approach to Ripon is

undoubtedly along the B6265, which passes only a mile or so north of Newby. From the road, Ripon Cathedral stands proud above the Ure Valley; once the city is reached, the cathedral disappears from view and its massive west front only confronts the surprised traveller leaving the centre along Kirkgate. The cathedral of St Peter and St Wilfrid used to present a dark and gloomy façade, scowling at prospective visitors, but cleaning has produced a new-build cathedral, almost too sparkling, as some magic has disappeared with the muck.

The Saxon crypt restores the atmosphere. It was built around 670 as part of the Benedictine monastery founded by Wilfrid, who took over as abbot after monks from Melrose has established the original community in the mid-seventh century. Although church and monastery were destroyed by the Danish King Eadred of Northumberland in 950, the crypt remained unscathed, and is now the oldest complete Saxon crypt in England. Rebuilding work on the church began around 1175-80, and the west front dates from 1120-30; inside, look for the misericords in the choir stalls.

Ripon itself is the second smallest city in England. Three hospitals were established in Ripon in medieval times, while the city's commercial success rested on agriculture, markets and textiles. The River Skell, which joins the Ure just east of Ripon, provided power for the mills. Much building took place in the seventeenth century, and the city developed to the north and west in the nineteenth century. Ripon is a brick-built city, with a pleasant, open market square. The lofty obelisk was erected in 1781 by William

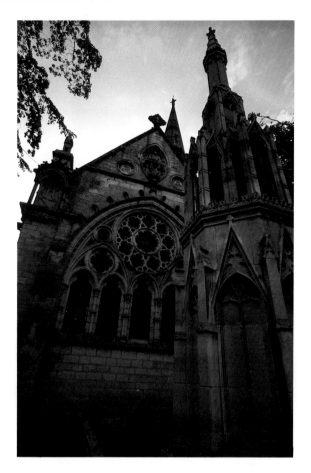

The church of Christ the Consoler at Skelton.

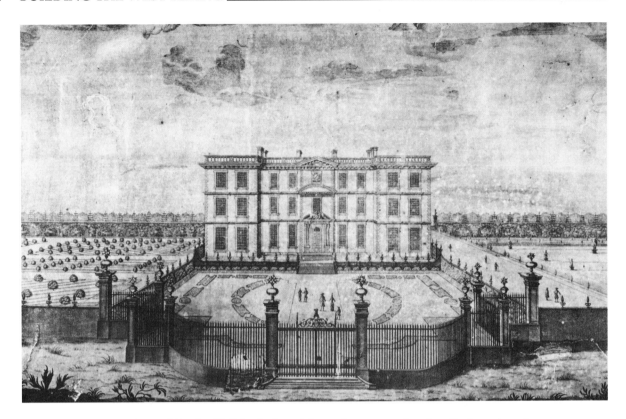

The west front of Newby Hall in the late eighteenth century, showing the formal gardens.

Newby Hall from the south-east, around 1830.

The west lodge of Kirby Hall, Little Ouseburn.

Aislabie of Studley Royal to commemorate his sixty year term as Member of Parliament for the city.

The terracotta façade of the 1905 swimming baths in Park Street is fun, and the traveller follows this road to find the Aislabie *tour de force*, the Studley Royal estate, a great eighteenth century green garden. One approach is via the footpath heading for Studley Roger, which leaves the road soon after the western edge of Ripon. The estate houses and gate lodges of Studley Roger loom across the fields, then the walker passes under a monumental triumphal arch with aggressive vermiculated rustication and hefty ball finials, and enters the Deer Park. St Mary's Church is directly ahead but, on turning, the first inkling of landscape manipulation is apparent: the lime avenue is aligned with the towers of Ripon Cathedral.

John Aislabie was a Yorkshireman, the son of a successful landowner and lawyer who had risen high at court. He became Chancellor of the Exchequer in 1714 but was ruined by the South Sea Bubble, the mania for joint stock investment in the Americas which indirectly funded the National Debt. When returns eventually failed to fulfil dizzy expectations in 1720, the Bubble burst and much money was lost, though few heads rolled. Aislabie was made a scapegoat and disqualified for life from public office, so retired to his Yorkshire estate and continued with his hugely ambitious plan to transform it into a visual and physical link between the medieval sites of Ripon Cathedral and Fountains Abbey. Thus he attempted to control the landscape after the financial world proved beyond his grasp.

He began work in 1716, inspired perhaps by architectural and horticultural contacts in London and Yorkshire, but maybe more by his work at Hall Barn in Buckinghamshire, a garden designed by his second wife's father Edmund Waller. Aislabie helped Colen

Campbell complete Hall Barn, a formal canal garden centred on Waller's house. At Studley Royal, Aislabie used funds from his estates and East India investments to employ over 100 men under gardener William Fisher. His plan was an unusual combination of French formal garden and English medievalism, a display of human domination of the landscape set between two beautiful and powerful pieces of human work for God.

Runnning through Studley Royal is the Skell, which Aislabie canalised, shaped into geometric pools, dammed to make a lake, and made the basis of a water garden. Vistas were opened up and eye-catcher after eye-catcher arose on the wooded hillsides, as Aislabie's taste turned more to the Picturesque in later years. He died in 1742 and work was continued by his son William, who concentrated on the upper reaches of the Skell near the ruin of Fountains Abbey. William Aislabie bought the Fountains Abbey estate in 1768, thus completing his father's vision, although views of the abbey had always been part of the picturesque experience of Studley Royal.

St Mary's Church was added to the estate in 1871-8, the commission coming to William Burges in the same year as that for Skelton church, 1870. Both churches were built in memory of Frederick Vyner, who was killed by Greek bandits; Skelton was erected by his mother, while St Mary was built by his brother-in-law Lord Ripon at the behest of Lady Ripon. The theme of the interior decoration at St Mary was 'Paradise Lost and Paradise Regained', which Burges interpreted using black marble, coloured alabasters, mosaics, porphyry (a hard, igneous rock, often purple and white), frescoes and stained glass. The cost of this elaborate memorial was around £50,000. Numerous paths take the walker to Fountains Abbey from St Mary's, all providing exquisite picturesque views of the water garden, architectural oddities and finally the abbey.

It is the largest monastic ruin in Britain, and to stroll through it is to visit a small village. Fountains Abbey was founded in 1132 by Benedictine monks who were dissatisfied with the laxity of the regime at their York monastery. They moved to the site beside the Skell and joined the Cistercian order in 1133, and two years later began to build a permanent home using local stone. By the end of the twelfth century there were probably more than 50 monks and at least 200 lay brothers at Fountains, and much building took place in the first half of the thirteenth century. In the fourteenth century Fountains was raided by the Scots and hit by the Black Death, but a final period of building followed in 1475 to 1528.

The abbey surrendered to Henry VIII on the 26th November 1539, and after the Dissolution was bought by Sir Richard Gresham, who rapidly stripped out all easily-saleable material. The site was sold to Sir Stephen Proctor in 1597, who used much of the stone to build Fountains Hall before selling the abbey and its lands to William Aislabie. The magnificent ruin was then in an ideal state of Picturesque decay, and Aislabie turfed the fields in which the ruin lay to produce the perfect picture.

At Fountains today the Skell still gurgles through channels beneath stone slabs, as the river was cunningly incorporated into the plan of the abbey to maximise its usefulness as both freshwater supply and drain. The rib-vaulted cellarium is over 300 feet long, and Huby's Tower, built about 1500 by Abbot Marmaduke Huby, is 170 feet high. Such a tower would have been unusual in an early Cistercian church, as their statutes forbade embellishment and aimed for simplicity and restraint in building. However, by the fifteenth century the order and its architecture had evolved: the Cistercians became more worldly and their buildings were suitably splendid.

The product of Sir Stephen Proctor's demolition of the abbey is but a few hundred yards to the west: Fountains Hall, one of the most fashionable houses in England when it was built around 1611. The architect was probably Robert Smythson, although it appears that he did not supervise the building work himself. Smythson designed the prodigy houses of Longleat and Hardwick, and Fountains Hall was one of his last works. Proctor, who made his fortune from coal and leadmining, was an extreme Protestant detested by his Yorkshire neighbours, who twice attempted to assassinate him. He doubtless enjoyed the irony inherent in the source of building stone for the hall.

A quarter mile north of the hall is the latest addition to the Fountains landscape, the National Trust Visitor Centre, opened in 1992 after six years of planning and construction. Edward Cullinan Architects designed a £2,000,000 quadrangle of timber and steel, with flying gables rising above a drystone wall base. The tip of the abbey tower may be seen from the centre, but from the valley the cunningly-sited new structure is invisible.

The traveller has now reached the end of the Studley Royal estate and its journey

Hackfall Woods, with Mowbray Castle in the distance.

through English architectural styles, though not the last of the Aislabie contributions to the landscape. Take the road south from Fountains Hall, which reveals a breathtaking view of the hall on the climb out of the valley, and head onwards for a mile to How Hill. Here, legend tells us, is where the Devil fired his four arrows towards Boroughbridge, but the Devil's Arrows fell short, and can now be found in a field just west of the town. No trace of the Devil's presence remains on How Hill, but the Chapel of St Michael de Monte occupies its summit.

Abbot Huby built the original chapel on this hilltop site, which itself has Saxon associations. The chapel fell into a ruined state after the Dissolution but was rebuilt by John Aislabie in 1718. Its use had changed from religion to recreation by 1737, when gaming tables were installed; the Picturesque was the coming fashion, and the hill was a fine spot from which to view the Aislabie estate. A permissive path exists to the hilltop ruin from the Fountains road, so now we can all enjoy the spectacular panorama.

A lane leads north-east from How Hill to Markenfield Hall, a fourteenth century moated manor house. Licence to crenellate was granted to John de Markenfield in 1310, but the family forfeited the hall after supporting Mary Stuart's claim to the throne. A small stone bridge crosses the moat and leads to a sixteenth century gatehouse; across the courtyard lies the L-shaped and battlemented hall, with its turreted stair-tower.

The traveller may walk west from Fountains Hall, following first the road then a two mile woodland track alongside the Skell leading to Spa Gill Woods. Here in 1698 a sulphur spring was found which attracted vast numbers of visitors in the summer, but lack of accommodation precluded nearby Aldfield becoming another Harrogate. The church of St Laurence at Aldfield, built around 1783, has a well-preserved three-tier pulpit and box pews.

The rising land to the north of the Ripon-Pateley Bridge road is cut through by tributaries of the Ure and criss-crossed by a warren of lanes and footpaths. Here the

The Rustic Temple at Fountain Plain, Hackfall Woods.

foothills of the Yorkshire Dales are dotted with towers. West of Kirkby Malzeard, the Greygarth Monument, on a hilltop a mile south of Swetton near Dallowgill Moor, is easily seen for miles around. East of Kirkby Malzeard the castellated Azerley Tower is

The Chapel of St Michael de Monte on How Hill.

harder to find, lurking on a hill half a mile east of Azerley village.

The boundary of the West Riding follows the course of the Ure upstream from below West Tanfield until after the river passes through Hackfall Woods, just north of Grewelthorpe, when the boundary heads westward. At Old Sleningford Hall, a mile south of West Tanfield, woodland and water gardens lie just south of the Ure. Further west at Grewelthorpe, paths lead indirectly into Hackfall Woods, which turn out to be another Aislabie confrontation with landscape - in fact, William Aislabie's very own garden. Although William tended and extended his father's design at Studley Royal, he was keen to experiment on his own terms, and started work at Hackfall in 1750.

He turned Hackfall Woods into a great romantic garden centred on Fountain Plain, a riverside park where promenaders could admire a mighty fountain and view from afar the picturesque buildings arranged on the valley side.

A path leads steeply down from the Grewelthorpe-Masham road through head-high bracken to what remains of the pond, with the Rustic Temple by its side. At Hackfall, Aislabie also built Fisher's Hall - an octagonal belvedere named for his head gardener - the sham ruin of Mowbray Castle, the banqueting house at Mowbray Point and many smaller conceits. This Georgian theme park attracted visitors until the early years of this century, but the cascade no longer falls and the structures are now derelict (though plans exist for their restoration). Even so, to walk through Hackfall Woods today is still to experience the heady combination of wealth and ideas at work on the natural landscape.

DANGEROUS CORNER AND THE VALLEY OF DESOLATION

Nidderdale and Wharfedale

For a panoramic view over the lower reaches of Wharfedale, Nidderdale and much more, climb Almscliff Crag. The crag is six miles south of Harrogate along the Bradford road (A658), just west of North Rigton village and but a mile away from Weeton Station; footpaths lead from the station or North Rigton to the crag.

The view takes in Harrogate to the north-east, Leeds and Bradford on the horizon south across the Wharfe, and to the west is rising ground, the edge of the Yorkshire Dales.

Descending to the countryside on a more intimate scale, a combination of footpaths and country lanes will take the traveller west towards Stainburn and the wooded Washburn Valley with its four reservoirs.

The Norman church of St Mary the Virgin is set outside the stone-built hamlet, on the road north to Braythorn. The churchyard looks out over Wharfedale and the church itself is small, more of a chapel. The porch is medieval and there are seventeenth century touches including a triangular headed window, but the building is still almost an unreconstructed Norman country church with a fine chancel arch. From this bleak edge of Stainburn Moor the village of Leathley is two miles south-west, with another Norman church, St Oswald, in which can be found the Percy crescent decorating capitals in the nave, and fine ironwork, maybe twelfth century, on the west door.

A footbridge over the Washburn, which enters the Wharfe a mile to the south, will take the walker towards Farnley; the road journey around Farnley Lake is longer, but the northern route is steep and spectacular as it climbs in and out of the valley. Farnley Hall, south of the village, is an Elizabethan structure with an excellent but severe John Carr house added to it in 1786-90 for Walter Fawkes. Internally, all is exquisite neo-Classical decoration with some fine fireplaces.

The steep-sided Washburn Valley runs north to Fewston, its reservoirs providing water for the people of Leeds. The whole area, partly wooded, is laced with footpaths and even river crossings are no more than a mile apart. The church of St Lawrence at Fewston was built in 1697, and now stands above Swinsty Reservoir.

Dangerous Corner is a mile north-east of Fewston, where the road north from Otley crosses the A59 Harrogate-Skipton road. The openness of this otherwise bleak part of the moors is compromised by the arcane and chilling shapes of the Menwith Hill radar domes. Four miles east along the A59 (a road to be avoided on a summer Sunday afternoon) is the turning north to Hampsthwaite, the River Nidd and the Nidderdale Way.

The church of St Thomas à Becket at Hampsthwaite was restored by Hodgson Fowler in 1902; inside it lies a florid, white marble effigy of composer Amy Woodforde-Finden, who died in 1919. She was born in Valparaiso in 1860, and her songwriting success came after marriage to an Indian Army officer in 1894. Her collections of sentimental melodies with Oriental or Indian subjects, beginning with *Four Indian Love Lyrics* in 1902, were popular during the early 1900s. The church lies on the banks of the Nidd, on the course of the Nidderdale Way. Beside it a bridge leads over the river towards Clint, and a right turn where the road bends west will take the traveller along a lane, a bridlepath and into Europe: the continental village of Ripley, with its Hotel de Ville, Schloss and admonition at the fifteenth century gatehouse to 'Parlez au Suisse'.

This unexpected incursion of foreignness into the West Riding was the work of William Ingilby, whose family had owned Ripley Castle since around 1350. Ingilby's architectural ideas were formed through his travels abroad, particularly to Germany. He was always equipped with a notebook in which to jot down plans and details of buildings, and Ripley village, begun around 1780, is a combination of very English estate cottages and enjoyable foreign follies. Terraces of mildly Tudor Gothic cottages are set off by the battlemented bulk of the highly Gothic Hotel de Ville of 1854, completed by Ingilby's wife after his death. The entire apparition took about eighty years to build, and complements the Schloss or Castle, rebuilt in 1827-8; in the garden is an elegant orangery.

The village church, All Saints, was rebuilt around 1395 after a landslide undercut its site. Restoration in 1862 gave the church examples of stained glass by several of the best designers of the time, including Clayton & Bell, William Wailes, William Warrington and Ward & Hughes. In the churchyard is the base of a medieval weeping cross, with eight niches where penitents may kneel and pray.

Upstream from Ripley, the ever-steepening valley of the Nidd runs north-west to Pateley Bridge, the route once followed by the railway from Harrogate's Starbeck Station. The land is dotted with farms and woodland, less populous now than in 1794 when it was reported to be entirely enclosed by small stone-walled fields, with tiny farms producing butter for the London market and oatmeal-fed hogs for London and Lancashire.

Several Nidderdale townships were once the property of Fountains Abbey, and its dissolution set off a chain of land-dealing and building lasting several centuries. Sir Richard Gresham bought the entire abbey estates for £10,122 18s 4d, twenty times their rent in 1540, and soon sold off half a dozen townships between Ripley and Pateley Bridge to Sir Arthur Darcy. Darcy held the lands for twenty years then sold on, in some cases to the tenants. Within one or two generations, these now-prosperous farmers began to replace their farmhouses with dwellings more suited to their station; this process also occurred outside Nidderdale. In addition, on Nidderdale estates where farms were leased for periods of 3,000 years, thus giving the same security as outright purchase, similar rebuilding took place.

Dacre lies west of the Nidd and five miles downstream from Pateley Bridge. It was one of the townships bought by Sir Arthur Darcy, and is notable for its church, Holy Trinity (1837), which is reputed to have been designed by 'a young lady of the neighbourhood'.

A track and footpath follow the Nidd up to the village of Glasshouses, which expanded from the 1850s around Glasshouses Mill, just to the south of the river bridge. The flax-spinning mill was built in 1812 on the site of a corn mill, and expanded after 1835 when it was bought by the Metcalfe family. A huge iron breastshot waterwheel, designed by leading mill engineers William Fairbairn & Sons of Manchester, was installed in 1850-1, and was the subject of a court case in 1854 when levels in the Nidd rose and adversely affected its performance. A mill dam retaining a ten million gallon reservoir eventually ensured continuous running of the wheel, which now resides at Quarry Bank Mill near Manchester.

Glasshouses Mill, which employed 264 people in 1851, acquired a steam engine in 1857 and a water turbine in 1871; the latter was replaced in the 1890s, with the turbine now visible from the gallery which occupies part of the ground floor. The mill was converted to hemp spinning in 1899. Although the imposing chimney stack was demolished in the early 1980s, the mill's low, brick-arched ceiling and iron columns combine with the vast scale of the remaining machinery to give a glimpse of factory life in the last century.

Just over a mile upstream stands Pateley Bridge, a market town since the fourteenth century and the ancient centre of Nidderdale. The Brigantes and then the Romans worked the lead deposits which run from near Pateley Bridge in a strip a few miles wide north-west across the high moors to Buckden in Wharfedale. Flax and linen industries also flourished here.

The town's narrow High Street plunges dramatically towards the Nidd crossing, leaving behind the parish church, St Cuthbert, built in 1827. High above the town up Old Church Lane are the ruins of St Mary's Church, dating from at least 1691; continuing along this road towards Kirkby Malzeard provides the traveller with wonderfully expansive views east over the Cleveland Hills. The view back over Nidderdale from Old Church Lane takes in the moorlands to the south-west, on which stand Yorke's Folly, a pair of ruined columns which would have been happier inside a cathedral. Also known as the Two Stoops, the ruins were built for John Yorke of Bewerley Hall in 1800; they were originally a trio, but one fell down in 1893. They provided work for the unemployed whilst under construction, and perhaps this was their sole purpose, although they are undoubtedly picturesque.

The Two Stoops are about two miles from the centre of Pateley Bridge. To inspect the

School Street, Pateley Bridge, in the early twentieth century.

clifftop ruins more closely, cross the Nidd in Pateley Bridge, take the lane leading south through Bewerley and begin the steep climb (by foot or road) south on to Heyshaw Moor at the second junction, just after a small bridge. After passing Skrikes Farm, several paths lead up from the road to the ruins, including one which forms the Nidderdale Way. From this moorland viewpoint, the Victorian villas of Pateley Bridge and the dale to the south may be seen below, although Gouthwaite Reservoir, one source of Bradford's water supply, lies just out of sight to the north-west. Two more reservoirs have been created above Middlesmoor, where the Nidd bends west.

A by-road follows the river upstream from

The Two Stoops (Yorke's Folly) above Pateley Bridge.

Pateley Bridge, running to the west of Gouthwaite Reservoir and crossing the Nidd twice before arriving at the small hill-village of Middlesmoor, half a mile north of How Stean Gorge on the eponymous Nidd tributary.

The church of St Chad looks south over Nidderdale, and was rebuilt in 1865-6 by William H Crossland, best known in Yorkshire for his work on the model industrial village of Akroydon in Halifax from 1861, although he also designed the magnificently ornate Gothic town hall at Rochdale (1866-71). A steep footpath (part of the Nidderdale Way) leads south-west half a mile downhill from close by the church to the gorge and Stean village.

West of Middlesmoor is moorland, with Great Whernside marking the eastern boundary of the Yorkshire Dales National Park and the beginning of the descent into Wharfedale. Footpaths linking Nidderdale and Wharfedale are few in this area, but serious walkers could take the Carle Fell Road leading west from Scar House Reservoir, then the bridlepath which ends at Starbotton after passing within half a mile of Nidd Head, source of the river.

Rather than beginning the exploration of Wharfedale in midstream, travellers wishing to start at the source of the river should make their way to Long Slack Gate, two miles north of Oughtershaw on the road leading south from Hawes into Langstrothdale, the upstream continuation of Wharfedale. (The roundabout route from Middlesmoor through Wensleydale takes the traveller into the North Riding, and Long Slack Gate lies on the West Riding boundary.) The panoramic view from this central point of the Dales Park is splendid.

Heading south, the road descends steeply towards the Wharfe, reaching the river just north of the hamlet of Oughtershaw. Small though it is, Oughtershaw boasts two memorials to Queen Victoria and a charming Romanesque village hall, erected in memory of Lydia Wilson Woodd, who died aged only thirty-two at Pau in the deepest south of France. From Oughtershaw, river and Dales Way now follow much the same course, the Dales Way starting in Ilkley and ending eighty miles north-west at Bowness-on-Windermere.

At Beckermonds the Wharfe turns south-east. Three miles distant is Hubberholme where the valley begins to widen, and the rustic twelfth century church of St Michael and All Angels houses a great rarity, the sole surviving rood loft in the West Riding. The church is the furthest upstream in Wharfedale and its rood loft, a gallery over the partition separating nave and choir, is dated 1558. On its east face is elegant Perpendicular tracery. Rood lofts were introduced in the fifteenth century, but many were destroyed in the Reformation.

Fine views of village and dale can be seen from the footpath along the crag tops to the north, part of a triangular walk connecting Hubberholme, Buckden and Cray which uses the Dales Way between Hubberholme and Buckden. An alternative lower-level route between Cray and Hubberholme takes in the pretty sequence of waterfalls along Cray Gill.

Two miles south of Kettlewell the River Skirfare meets the Wharfe, though walkers may cross the ridge separating Wharfedale from Littondale, the valley of the Skirfare, by several routes. A bridlepath links Buckden and Litton, and another crosses Old Cote

Moor between Starbotton and the beautiful village of Arncliffe.

Starbotton was almost completely destroyed by flooding from Cam Gill Beck in 1686, but was rebuilt in the eighteenth and nineteenth centuries as a consequence of the rise of the leadmining industry.

Arncliffe Church was reconstructed in 1841 by the prolific Newcastle-upon-Tyne architect John Dobson, and contains an east window of 1847 with stained glass by Newcastle glazier William Wailes.

South-west of Arncliffe, Brootes Lane runs south of a visible Celtic field system and climbs the valley of Cowside Beck, a sheer and craggy introduction to the limestone outcrops of Malham Moor.

Back in Wharfedale, the precipitous limestone scar of Kilnsey Crag overshadows the village of Kilnsey, in the hands of monks from Fountains Abbey from 1156 and used as a court and sheep-shearing centre. The hulking eyebrow of the crag is much used by multicoloured climbers who amazingly adhere to unlikely positions beneath the overhang.

Grassington is the first substantial settlement in Wharfedale to be met by the traveller arriving from the remote reaches of the upper dale. The village held a market in medieval times, and was a leadmining centre between the seventeenth and nineteenth centuries. The Old Hall, originally the manor house, dates partly from the thirteenth century, and there are several seventeenth century stone cottages.

Over the Wharfe is Linton, where Linton Beck trickles through the village green under packhorse and clapper bridges, and stepping

The Dawson tombstone, designed and carved by Eric Gill, in the churchyard of St Wilfrid, Burnsall.

stones or a ford offer other routes across. At the end of the green stands Fountaine's Hospital, an edifice comprising seven almshouses for poor women built in 1721 by an unknown architect. The donor was Richard Fountaine. The Classical design is clearly not a vernacular product, and even Vanburgh has been suggested as the culprit. Linton Church, St Michael, is delightfully situated

The church of St Michael at Linton, across the River Wharfe.

on the riverbank about half a mile to the north-east of the village.

Across the river the Dales Way leads downstream to Burnsall, where Eric Gill's work unexpectedly features in the churchyard of St Wilfrid on a tombstone dedicated to the Dawson family, lords of the manor of Hartlington and great church benefactors. Gill, a family friend, carved the stone in 1934 while staying at the Dawson's home Hartlington Hall, half a mile east of Burnsall Bridge. It takes the form of a crucifix with elegant lettering and stands to the east of the chancel. The oldest part of the substantial and attractive church of St Wilfrid dates from 1140, with further building taking place in 1520-40 and 1612, and restoration in 1858-9. Its most intriguing feature is the centrally-

Looking towards Wharfedale from Parcevall Hall.

The chapel garden at Parcevall Hall.

pivoted lychgate, a surprise for first-time visitors.

Four miles east of Burnsall along the Appletreewick road is Parcevall Hall, a fifteenth century farmhouse which originally belonged to Bolton Priory. It was almost a ruin when bought by London architect Sir William Milner in 1927, but over the following thirty years he extended the house and created an intriguing garden on the inhospitable hillside. After his death in 1960 the garden was allowed to deteriorate, but recent work has restored the delights of its Arts and Crafts style terraces and views over Wharfedale. The orchard, a woodland garden and - close to the hall - a courtyard garden with a tiny chapel, complete an unusual piece of twentieth century garden design. The overwhelming feeling is one of tranquility. Walk up through the terraces, where perfectly-placed seats demand delay, to reach the brilliantly-colourful borders near the hall, and turn for a splendid view topped by craggy Simons Seat.

At Burnsall Bridge the traveller enters the outrageously picturesque Bolton Abbey Estate, which ends seven miles to the south along the meanders of the Wharfe at Bolton Bridge. The river may be crossed on stepping stones near Drebley, and by road at Barden Bridge, built in 1659. The beautiful ruin of Barden Tower stands to the south-west of the bridge on the B6160. It was a three-storey tower house built in 1485 by Henry, Lord Clifford, and restored in 1658-9 by Lady Anne Clifford, Countess of Pembroke, who domesticated the tower by adding large windows on the south face.

The Clifford family were also deeply involved with the development of the Bolton Abbey estate, which centres on Bolton Priory in its idyllic situation within a bend of the Wharfe at Bolton-in-Wharfedale. This Augustinian priory was founded at Embsay, four miles west of Bolton, in 1120-1 by William Meschin and his wife Cecilia de Rumilly. The unproductive Embsay site could not support the canons, and new patroness Alice de Rumilly, daughter of William and Cecilia, consented to the move to Bolton which took place in 1154-5.

The Austin canons, as they were known in England, were popular in lay society; not only were their houses easy to found, but they were a relatively conservative order fitting in well with established society. Neither missionary nor evangelical but assuming a pastoral role, they were an accepted part of English medieval life. The number of canons at Bolton usually stood at around fifteen, a typically small Austin house, and after a series of early fourteenth century Scottish raids, several canons had to find temporary homes elsewhere. The destruction wrought by the Scots did, however, result in fine rebuilding work at the priory.

The original priory church was built in the late twelfth and mid to late thirteenth centuries, and its nave survives in use today as the parish church. The chancel, its huge Gothic windows minus their tracery, was built almost entirely in the second quarter of the fourteenth century, after the Scots had done their worst. The ornate west tower, begun in 1520, was the last addition to the church before suppression of the priory in 1539, and there are also remains of monastic buildings, notably the octagonal chapter house. Sadly, the priory's wooded valley setting turns from sublime to ridiculous in summer when crowds flock to the riverbank as if to Blackpool beach. In the depths of winter when the Wharfe becomes a torrent, the priory is desolate but romantic.

West of the priory church is Bolton Hall, essentially the early fourteenth century priory gatehouse with later wings to either side. The south wing was added in 1720 and the north wing dates from 1843, the latter possibly being the work of Joseph Paxton. The hall is a home of the Duke of Devonshire; after the Dissolution the Bolton Abbey estate was purchased by the Cliffords of Skipton, and passed by marriage to the Earl of Burlington and thence the Duke of Devonshire.

Paths lead down either bank of the Wharfe from Barden Bridge towards the priory, and, half a mile downstream, walkers may cross the river on a jolly castellated bridge, originally an aqueduct.

Soon the going underfoot becomes more treacherous and the walker comes upon the Strid, where the valley closes in to crush the

Edwardian visitors crossing the Wharfe by stepping stones at Bolton Abbey.

The terrace gardens at Parcevall Hall.

1843. Around thirty miles of paths were laid out between Barden Bridge and the priory, viewpoints were constructed and seats provided.

Half a mile downstream from the Strid near Posforth Bridge, a permissive path leads north through the Valley of Desolation to Simons Seat, a millstone grit outcrop on the highest point of Barden Fell, by way of a path through Bolton Abbey estate access land (this is not always open to walkers). The Valley of Desolation acquired its name after a damaging storm in 1826, but now the gill, two waterfalls and tree-lined slopes contradict the stark image.

On the roadside below Strid Woods on the west bank stands the Cavendish Memorial, a hexagonal Gothic fountain erected in 1886 by the electors of the West Riding in memory of Frederick Charles Cavendish, son of the seventh Duke of Devonshire. He was appointed Chief Secretary for Ireland by Gladstone in 1882, and was stabbed to death in Dublin that same year by an extremist group known as the Invincibles. The architects of this monumental fountain were Worthington & Elgood of Manchester; Thomas Worthington designed Manchester's Albert Memorial in 1862-7.

To avoid the busy junction at Bolton Bridge, cross the Wharfe by the footbridge just below the priory, and head for Storiths before taking the footpath south to Beamsley. It meets the A59 almost beside the most unusual almshouses known as Beamsley Hospital. An archway through the row of almshouses on the main road leads into the garden, where stands a circular stone building thirty feet in diameter, its central lantern guarded by four

This castellated aqueduct crosses the Wharfe half a mile downstream from Barden Bridge.

river between walls only 6 to 8 feet apart. Such is the short distance across the cascade that the temptation to jump has proved too great for many, and the resulting fatalities include the son of Alicia de Rumilly. The area surrounding the Strid was developed into something of a Picturesque pleasure-ground by local vicar William Carr between 1789 and tall chimney-stacks. This was the original almshouse building, erected in 1593 by Margaret, Countess of Cumberland. The rooms are arranged around a central chapel, through which most of the seven almswomen had to pass to reach their rooms. The roadside range was added about 1650-60 by Lady Anne Clifford, daughter of the countess.

There are precedents for the circular form in religious buildings, for instance the churches of the Knights Templar, which were modelled on the rotunda of the Church of the Holy Sepulchre in Jerusalem, but perhaps Beamsley Hospital was simply the fanciful product of Elizabethan exhibitionism. It was used for its original purpose until the 1970s and is now owned by the Landmark Trust, its oddly-shaped rooms available as holiday accommodation.

Crossing the A59, a footpath leads south into Beamsley village. Many routes into Ilkley are then possible along the valley side to the north of the Wharfe using the network of by-roads and footpaths. The countryside on this moorland fringe is peculiarly quiet considering the proximity of the conurbation. The B6160 provides a more direct approach to Ilkley, and a mile south of Bolton Bridge passes Farfield Hall, built for the Myers family in 1728 but now in institutional use. The highly-decorative Baroque stone façade includes sea monsters, shells and giant Corinthian pilasters.

Ilkley is a return from the rigorous and picturesque delights of Wharfedale to civilization or reality, depending on taste, but at least the spa town has retained a functioning railway station. A settlement has existed at Ilkley since Roman times, but the town came

to prominence as the result of the discovery of mineral springs. The Middelton family from Myddelton Lodge, on the north bank of the Wharfe opposite Ilkley, built a bath house supplied by these waters at White Wells, on the slopes of Ilkley Moor, in 1699. It took almost a century and a half for Ilkley to become fashionable, but by the 1840s it was a flourishing resort, and many of its most imposing buildings date from the late Victorian or Edwardian periods. Although something of a miniature Harrogate, with canopied shops and Scottish Baronial style hotels, the town's late Victorian suburban architecture in its delightfully lush setting gives Ilkley a most unusual character.

The Otley & Ilkley Joint Railway arrived at Ilkley in 1865, by which time the town was an expanding dormitory for Leeds and Bradford. The line was extended to Skipton in 1888, but this portion closed in 1965 and the single-storey Italianate station, designed by J H Sanders, is once more a terminus, used by trains from Leeds. Opposite the station is the town hall, a complex of public offices, assembly room, winter gardens and library built in 1906-8 by Leeds architect William Bakewell, who won the commission in competition.

The old town lies to the west of the station near the river, and is centred on All Saints Church, built partly on the site of Olicana Roman fort, founded around AD 79. The wooden fort was reconstructed in stone in the second century, but was abandoned by the fifth century, whereupon the church was built (and rebuilt) using material from the fortifications. The oldest visible part of All Saints is the thirteenth century south doorway;

The church of St Michael and All Angels at Hubberholme, upper Wharfedale.

the church was almost completely rebuilt in 1860-1.

The first of the town's substantial spa buildings was the Ben Rhydding Hydropathic Establishment built in 1843-4 in the Scottish Baronial style. It has long since been demolished but Wells House, a towered hotel-cum-baths erected in 1858, is now the college of education. Cuthbert Brodrick designed Wells House in the year he completed Leeds Town Hall, and went on to build the massive Scarborough Grand Hotel in 1863-7.

Ilkley's population grew as it became a popular residential area for the traders of Leeds and Bradford and their employees, and a property and building boom resulted in the 1870s. Many suburban villas of this period still remain, especially along Queens Drive where moorland meets town, a surreal conjunction for backpacking walkers.

A wide variety of architectural styles appealed to the wealthy merchants, who generally commissioned Leeds or Bradford architects to produce their dream homes. Richard Norman Shaw worked in the West Riding from the 1860s, and in Ilkley built the Tudor mansion of St Johns in 1878-9. Other notable villas in the Queens Drive area include Woodbank, 1870s Gothic by Thomas Ambler, the Italianate Arden Lea, and neighbouring Arden Croft (1897) by Thomas C Hope in the Old English style made famous by Richard Norman Shaw. These Ilkley suburbs are a happy combination of severe, dark stonework with architectural felicities and generous gardening.

Edwin Lutyens built Heathcote, on Kings Road, the antidote to this decorative domesticity in 1906-8. He was commissioned by Bradford merchant Ernest Hemingway, and was not impressed by the 'dreadful kind' of villas surrounding the site. He produced a Classical design of great power in a stripped Baroque style using York stone and red pantiles. Lutyens also designed the gardens and all the furniture, and chose the carpets and curtains. Although the house is now used as offices, many original features of the Lutyens interior remain. Heathcote epitomised the movement in English architecture away from Victorian excess towards the cool Classical style and eventually the starkness of the Modern movement.

Many paths lead from the fringe of Ilkley on to the moors to the south. To the west is the wooded ravine of Hebers Ghyll, leading up to the Swastika Stone by Woodhouse Crag. This is a powerful Bronze Age carving; the swastika is an ancient motif, once denoting good luck. This area of moorland has many other Bronze Age remains, including the Twelve Apostles, a stone circle on the Dales Way link with Bradford which leads south from Ilkley.

There is no riverside path between Ilkley and Otley, but walkers may use the Dales Way link to Leeds which passes through the commuter village of Menston, then follows the Chevin, the 925 foot high scarp slope to the south of Otley. There are spectacular views and an exciting stepped walk down into the town from Mid-Chevin. Otley, a market town serving the surrounding agricultural area, has two outstanding and contrasting architectural attractions, both churches. The Norman parish church of All Saints and the Congregational church (1899) stand on the route from Mid-Chevin to the medieval bridge over the Wharfe.

All Saints has a Norman north doorway and chancel windows, though the bulk of the church dates from the fourteenth and fifteenth centuries. A later restoration was responsible for the richly decorative Arts and Crafts style wooden reredos. In the churchyard is a monument to the twenty-three navvies who died during the construction of the Leeds & Thirsk Railway tunnel under Bramhope Moor, four miles south-east of Otley. The monument is a pair of scaled-down copies of the turreted northern tunnel entrance, joined by a short tunnel length; the whole is castellated and about six foot in height, more adventure playground castle than memorial. The Bramhope Tunnel, still used by the Leeds-Harrogate line, was built in 1845-9 by engineer Thomas Grainger. It is over two miles long and runs 280 feet below ground at its deepest; during construction, more than 1,500 million gallons of water had to be pumped out of the workings to prevent flooding.

Otley's cathedral-like Congregational church, close to the river bridge, was built in 1899 by Bradford architects and brothers Thomas and Francis Healey, who specialised in ecclesiastical work. The severe, towered west front overlooks the roadside.

Across the bridge and just over a mile to the west along the Askwith road is Weston Hall, the Elizabethan home of the Vavasour family, partly rebuilt in the nineteenth century. The rare detached banqueting house stands in what was the walled garden; the decorative three-storey pleasure pavilion was built by Sir Mauger le Vavasour in the late sixteenth century.

From Otley the A660 Leeds road or the Dales Way link will take the traveller to

Ilkley Winter Gardens in the late 1930s, drawn by an unknown artist.

Bramhope, where another architectural rarity is to be found, one of the few ecclesiastical buildings to be erected during the Commonwealth - Bramhope Chapel. It stands on the Leeds road on the western edge of Bramhope, close to the Dales Way link route, a plain and unobtrusive single-storey stone building with mullioned windows and a bellcote. It was built by 'ardent and unswerving Puritan' Richard Dyneley on his Bramhope estate in 1649. Inside, the box pews are arranged to focus on the three-decker pulpit. Staircase Lane, an old packhorse road, leads off the main road almost immediately north of the chapel, and after a quarter mile or so a footpath heads east and down the scarp to a wooded valley. Those wishing to glimpse the full-size version of the Bramhope Tunnel entrance, a fine castellated railway eccentricity, should follow this path and peer south through the woods into the cutting.

The railway crosses the Wharfe by viaduct a mile north of the tunnel entrance, but few footpaths exist in these riverside meadows. The A659 from Otley passes under the railway, through Arthington village and in a mile east reaches Arthington Nunnery, a beautiful three-storey stone house with row upon row of mullioned windows. It was built in 1585 using material from the Cluniac house founded at Arthington in 1154-5. The Cluniac order, with its highly-centralised administration, was not a great success in Britain; Arthington's complement was twelve nuns and a prioress, the small number by no means unusual for a nunnery. Their buildings were demolished within forty years of the suppression of the house in 1540.

From the nunnery the road continues east towards magnificent Harewood House, running alongside its park wall and dramatically climbing the steep bank overlooked by the substantial ruins of Harewood Castle before entering Harewood, the model village rebuilt outside the park around 1760.

Building on the Harewood estate began in the twelfth century with the castle, which was later rebuilt by Sir William Aldburgh; his daughters married Sir Richard Redmayne and Sir William Ryther, and these two families occupied the castle in the fifteenth century. Thomas Wentworth, Earl of Strafford, held part of the estate in the seventeenth century, including Gawthorp Hall, built for the Gascoigne family, which took the place of the castle. The hall stood to the south of the present Harewood House.

The estate was inherited by Strafford's son, a spendthrift who squandered his property and sold Gawthorp to the renowned miser Sir John Cutler; after passing through other hands, the entire Harewood estate was eventually purchased in 1739 by wealthy Yorkshireman Henry Lascelles, whose fortune came from the ribbon trade and interests in Barbados and the East India Company.

Henry's son Edwin inherited Harewood in 1753, but was previously much involved in running the estate as he acted as agent for his father during the late 1740s. On taking over the property, Edwin Lascelles altered and redecorated Gawthorp Hall, although he had already decided to build anew on a site with improved aspect. He obtained plans for a new mansion from John Carr in 1758, discussed and amended them with his architectural connoisseur friends, and finally allowed Carr to begin building in 1759.

Lascelles' new mansion, Harewood House, is a Palladian pile with a nine-bay central block and three-bay links to side pavilions; the north façade has giant attached Corinthian columns and a massive carved pediment. The neo-Classical interior design by Robert Adam was carried out in 1765-71, and Gawthorp Hall was demolished on completion of this exquisite scheme.

Meanwhile, Edwin Lascelles' urge to renew had spread unconfined through the entire Harewood estate. At his request, around 1760 Carr began to rebuild the old village of Harewood outside the park boundary, the new Classical cottages with their blank arch motif providing a fitting setting for the gateway to the house. This enterprise, which came to include a ribbon factory, inns and a school, was completed only around 1803. About that time the main lodge, a triumphal arch, was built at the head of the avenue leading through the village from Collingham. The original design was by Humphry Repton, but mason John Muschamp, son of the master mason who had built Harewood, was the eventual architect.

There was no attempt to move the village church, All Saints, which remained alone inside the park walls. It was built around 1410, much altered in 1793, probably to the designs of John Carr, and restored by Sir George Gilbert Scott in 1862-3. It is remarkable mainly for its collection of six family monuments dating from 1419 to 1510, which reveal the development of carving, clothing and funerary design during that period. The memorials include alabaster effigies of Sir William Ryther and his wife, and Sir Richard Redmayne. Redmayne's feet rest on a lion, while a beadsman - a man required to pray for others - insinuates himself between feet and animal.

Lancelot 'Capability' Brown worked on the park during 1772-81, enlarging the lake and opening up views of Wharfedale and Almscliff Crag to produce one of his best creative landscapes; the cost was £6,000. The south façade of the house was remodelled in 1843 by Sir Charles Barry, who also built the Italianate terraced garden with its three fountain pools. Later alterations to the house include the redesign of a dressing room in 1930-1 by Sir Herbert Baker, who with Edwin Lutyens was the architect of New Delhi. Although Harewood now means zoo, garden centre and adventure playground, nothing can compromise its sublime views and opulent architecture. Ribbons and sugar brought wealth to the Lascelles and high fashion to eighteenth century Wharfedale.

THE MIDLAND, THE MILLIONAIRE AND THE MANUFACTURERS

Airedale, Ribblesdale and the Three Peaks

It takes some minutes for your eyes to adjust to the gloom inside, but when the entire 120 foot length is visible, with its strapping king-posts and tie beams, the effect is overpowering. The Great Barn at East Riddlesden Hall, on the River Aire just north of Keighley, was built around 1640-50. It is an eight-bay aisled barn, with the aisles marked out by stout oak supports on stone bases.

East Riddlesden Hall stands on the site of a medieval house, and dates mainly from 1648 with a north-east wing built in 1692. The façade displays a memorable eight-spoke rose window, and the magnificent hall fireplace has an incongruous tiny fireplace sited directly above it. This was originally intended as the fireplace for the floor above, but open halls were becoming fashionable in the mid-seventeenth century, to impress visitors and use for semi-public events, and the upper room was never completed.

Both the dining parlour and gentleman-owner John Murgatroyd's private parlour have richly-ornamented ceilings, and the entire hall is full of fireplaces, even in the attic where the servants slept amongst the heavy roof timbers. East Riddlesden shows how the functions of the middling gentry house were changing during the seventeenth century: rooms became private, more specialised and more comfortable.

The grounds of East Riddlesden, including a walled garden and a monastic fishpond, run down to the River Aire. On the south bank lies Keighley, stretching along the valley of the River Worth, which leaves the Aire just west of the hall. The town centre is only a mile or so away by road, but a more interesting approach from East Riddlesden is to cross the old Bradford road and walk a few yards north to the Leeds & Liverpool Canal, which runs roughly parallel to the Aire. It was completed in 1816 and encouraged industrial development throughout Airedale.

The canal and towpath run west, first through Riddlesden, then at the foot of steeply rising moorland; in two miles, a footpath crosses a canal bridge and takes the walker south-west, through a golf course and beside the club house, towards the Skipton road. Cross the Aire and the road to find the entrance to Utley Cemetery almost immediately to the left. The cemetery, its once-secluded setting now a little compromised by the trunk road, is a rambling memorial to the manufacturers who made Victorian Keighley.

Utley Cemetery was founded in 1856 and laid out in terraces which step down to the railway cutting; this was bridged in 1910 when the cemetery was extended across the tracks. There are two entrance lodges and a Gothic chapel, but most notable are the ornate monuments to the town's industrial worthies, particularly the Butterfields who have their own family chapel and vault opposite the main gate. This miniature Gothic pile, built in the 1870s and now somewhat decrepit, is but an appetiser for the major Butterfield contribution to Keighley's architecture, the family home, Cliffe Castle. It stands in Spring Gardens Lane, but the walker may wander up to the castle through its grounds, via a gate in the massive walls less than half a mile west of the main cemetery entrance.

The first house on the site of the Castle was Cliffe Hall, a Tudor pile built for Keighley lawyer Christopher Netherwood in 1828-33. The Butterfield family, successful worsted spinners, manufacturers and exporters, rented the house in the 1840s then purchased it in 1848. Henry Isaac Butterfield (1819-1910) inherited the hall in 1874, and almost immediately began to transform it with the assistance of Bradford architect George Smith. The impetus for this work - the first stage of which was concluded in 1878 when the hall was renamed Cliffe Castle - may have come from Butterfield's wife Mary Roosevelt Burke. Though American, she had strong French family connections and the couple spent much time in Paris.

Smith added two towers, a reception room and a massive winter garden, but, not satisfied with this modest display of wealth, Butterfield extended the castle again around 1880 with two more towers, a ballroom, billiard room and library, all designed by local architect Wilson Bailey. To the winter garden he added a glass dome which reached a height of sixty-five feet. Two of the castle's four towers were around eighty feet high.

The interior of the castle was brilliantly colourful, and heavy with French influence and *objets d'art*; the upholstery and hangings were especially sumptuous. Leroux of Paris painted the ceilings, French-woven carpets were installed, and even the library was stocked with French books. The overall interior decoration was by Harland & Son, and Greenard of Paris, and included polished alabaster, intricate stonework, gilding, and colourful silks and satins. One stained glass window showed the entire Butterfield family, past and present, in Elizabethan dress. The architect was also remembered: George Smith's portrait was carved in the entrance hall stonework.

Despite all the effort and expenditure put into these improvements, Henry and his wife spent little time at the castle, preferring their houses in Paris and Nice, or simply touring. Their only son, Frederick Butterfield, inherited the castle in 1910, but he had never approved of his father's extravagance and let the house begin to decay. By the time of his death in 1943 it was in a poor state of repair, so bad that when it was bought and presented to the town in 1950 by local benefactor Sir Bracewell Smith, three towers had to be taken down during its conversion to museum use. Although the impact of the house has been diminished, it is still a forceful reminder of the confident spirit of the late Victorian manu- facturers.

The town of Keighley is largely a product of late eighteenth and nineteenth century growth, based on the production of textiles and machines for the textile trade. A gritty area of mills survives just east of the station, and local architectural peculiarities include the use of a wildly over-emphasised gable. Its Baroque form ornaments the old Cycling Club premises (1896) in Cavendish Street, where the shops are shaded by a pleasant if rather heavy-handed glass canopy. Cavendish Street leads from near the station to the town's main thoroughfare, North Street, where the Carnegie Library (1902-4) displays jolly Baroque decoration on its façade.

Keighley Station, with its spacious and happily old-fashioned booking hall, connects the restored Keighley & Worth Valley Railway into the main railway system. Regular steam-hauled services run up the Worth Valley to the terminus at Oxenhope, passing through Ingrow, Oakworth and Haworth.

Ingrow is best known for the Knowle Spring Brewery of Timothy Taylor & Company, founded in 1858 and housed in sandstone buildings dating from the 1860s and 1918. At Oakworth stood another vast Victorian mansion complete with fashionable winter garden, this one belonging to textile millionaire Sir Isaac Holden. All that remains of Oakworth House, an Italianate pile, is the

The Butterfield Chapel in Utley Cemetery, Keighley.

portico and the delightful gardens, Oakworth Park. The park was created in 1864-74 by French and Italian workmen, who built caves, grottoes, a hanging garden, a cascade and a summerhouse; most of this jolly pleasure garden is still intact.

Haworth can be grim, its grey stone cottages clinging to the side of a steep bank topped by church and parsonage. The parsonage, built around 1800 and once the home of 'Currer, Ellis and Acton Bell', is now a museum, a veritable Brontë shrine. Patrick Brontë, father of the sisters, was curate of St Michael's Church during 1820-61, but he would have known a simpler church, a basic, plain, stone box albeit with an earlier tower. This unloved eighteenth century structure was rebuilt in 1880, although the tower was left untouched.

The only escape from the crowds which throng Haworth may be to walk the Bronte Way west on to Haworth Moor, towards the Pennine Way and Lancashire. Several tracks and roads lead south from this path towards Oxenhope and the railway.

A variety of circuitous moorland routes take the driver from the Worth Valley back towards Airedale, perhaps heading north through Goose Eye and Laycock, whose architecture is typical of eighteenth century Pennine villages with income based on farming and the woollen industry.

West of Laycock, a winding by-road follows the valley of North Beck towards Cowling (on the A6068) via New Bridge. Half a mile past New Bridge is Earl Crag, over 1,000 feet above sea level. A short footpath from the road takes the walker to the ridge and the castellated Lund's Tower (or Sutton Pinnacle); an internal spiral stair leads upwards to a splendid panoramic viewpoint, with Airedale to the east and the ominous form of Pendle Hill in the west.

Lund's Tower was built by James Lund of Malsis Hall, a mile or so to the north-east near Glusburn. As to its purpose, it may have been yet another jubilee monument dedicated to Queen Victoria, or a family memorial connected with Lund's daughter Ethel. A footpath leads half a mile west along the crag top to Wainman's Pinnacle, a slightly lesser tower erected by the Wainman family of Carr Head, down in the valley below to the north, probably to commemorate victory at Waterloo; it was rebuilt in 1900.

Beyond Earl Crag the road descends steeply to the A6068, which drops down into Airedale just north of Sutton-in-Craven. Sutton's industrial past is revealed by the presence of mill buildings and the arched gateway of Sutton House, the Jacobean-style sole remains of a Victorian millowner's mansion. This jolly, turreted pair of lodges stand guard over Hall Drive, at the south-western corner of Sutton (off West Lane), and pretty remnants of garden buildings lie on the path beyond, which leads towards Sutton Moor.

Skipton lies four miles to the north, directly via the A629, or more picturesquely along rural roads at the foot of the moors to the west of the Aire, passing through Cononley and crossing the river at Carleton Bridge. The centre of Skipton is dominated by the bulbous twin towers of the castle gatehouse. The original Skipton Castle was built around 1090 by Robert de Romille to guard the gap breached in the Pennines by the Aire, but of this structure only an arch and gatehouse towers remain.

The present castle, a remarkably well-preserved specimen, dates from 1310 and the coming of the Clifford family, who owned the castle until the death of Lady Anne Clifford in 1676. The mighty gatehouse defends the south of the castle, while to the north a sheer cliff falls to Eller Beck. At the centre of the castle is Conduit Court, a fortified space on the domestic scale, and inside the fourteenth century main gate is one great surprise, the Shell Room. This is a grotto room dating from the 1620s which is lined with pearly shells from Guernsey and Jamaican coral. These seventeenth century souvenirs were brought home to Skipton by the third Earl of Cumberland, George Clifford, after expeditions abroad.

A settlement existed at Skipton in the Bronze Age, but the town really began to grow when the castle was built, bringing a garrison and the need for a market. This was established south of the castle at the top of High Street in 1204, and continued as the focus for development into the fourteenth and fifteenth centuries. The town became both market and industrial centre, its inhabitants including cloth-makers and dealers as well as merchants. The seventeenth century brought prosperity and the rebuilding of many High Street properties in stone. Lady Anne Clifford, born at Skipton Castle in 1590, rebuilt its somewhat decaying structure after 1655. Great changes came upon the town as a consequence of the arrival of the Leeds & Liverpool Canal in 1774.

The Springs Canal was cut from the main canal alongside Eller Beck to provide access to the limestone quarry at Haw Park, via a tramway. The stone was carried away eastwards and burnt in canalside kilns to produce lime for the agricultural and building trades. However, Skipton's main industry turned out to be the production of worsted, a fine wool fabric, which flourished from the early to mid-nineteenth century when the canal banks were lined with mills and weaving sheds. Today the mix of High Street façades presents a happily varied backdrop to the castle and Holy Trinity Church, restored (of course) by Lady Anne Clifford and with an unusual octagonal Jacobean font cover.

Skipton Station stands well below the town centre in the Aire Valley; it was built in 1876 by the Midland Railway and is one of the connecting stations between Keighley and Settle, and thence Carlisle on the famous Settle & Carlisle line, the Midland's route to Scotland, which opened in 1875. Skipton Station is a handsome stone building showing the Midland's symbol of a wyvern (a relative of the dragon) in a stone panel on the façade. Iron and glass ridge-and-furrow awnings, on decorative ironwork supports, cover both platforms.

Although the line from Skipton to Ilkley is now closed, its central section remains in operation as the Embsay Steam Railway. Embsay is two miles north-east of Skipton by road, and the station, opened by the Midland Railway in 1888, lies below the village; tank engines now haul trains east to rural Holywell Halt. To the north of Embsay the moors rise steeply, and in the lee of the reservoir above the village is to be found one of the most memorable place names in the West Riding: the hamlet of Good Intent.

West of Skipton, road, railway, canal, towpath and footpaths all take the traveller to

Conduit Court, Skipton Castle.

Skipton Castle.

Gargrave, a busy junction with several teashops beloved by the hordes of brilliantly-clothed cyclists who whirr through the village on Sunday afternoons, avoiding Pennine Way walkers and their packs.

A mile north stands neo-Jacobean Eshton Hall, visible from the Grassington road; the architect was young George Webster of Kendal, who built the impressive pile for Matthew Wilson in 1825-7. Webster, son of a Kendal builder and marble mason, was an early exponent of the neo-Jacobean style for country houses. This style became his speciality, although he also produced Classical public buildings and Gothic churches. He worked at Broughton Hall, two miles south of Gargrave, in 1838-41, making alterations to the existing house for Sir Charles Tempest. Webster was mayor of Kendal in 1829-30 when aged only thirty-three.

An easy stretch of the Pennine Way runs north from Gargrave, taking the walker across the canal and along a country lane bordered by the grounds of Gargrave House, before climbing gently over Eshton Moor. The path rejoins the Aire at Airton, where solid mill buildings line the west bank.

In the village, on the north side of the road leading from the bridge, a fine example of a carved Dales doorway datestone is to be found, the letters EWA being combined with the date 1696 on a lintel. These datestones are common throughout the Dales on houses of the seventeenth and eighteenth centuries, and vary from plain to highly decorative. The material is usually millstone grit and the date is normally that of the doorway itself, though it may refer to the entire house or major alterations. The initials are often those of the family surname at the top with the husband's and wife's christian names below.

The Pennine Way follows the Aire to Malham via Hanlith, where the house Badger Hill is ornamented by a bronze of St Francis of Assisi and a jolly badger weather-vane. Opposite is Hanlith Hall, which boasts a 1668 datestone (itself not visible from the road), but the hall was rebuilt in 1892.

For an early view of Malham Cove, the sheer limestone cliff created by the Craven Fault, take the road from Airton towards Kirkby Malham then a footpath west up Warber Hill; the cove can be seen in the northern distance, before the path turns to drop down into Kirkby Malham.

Here the church of St Michael the Archangel was built around 1490, though much has been added to the original structure. The style is Craven Perpendicular and the stone is millstone grit; on the south-west buttress of the tower are carved four coats of arms, including those of the Tempests of Broughton. The niches in the nave aisle-pillars, which once held statues of saints, appear only in Dales churches where the Tempests were the major benefactors. There are fine dated family and box pews, and an eleventh century font with strong primitive carving. The chancel panelling, by country house architect Guy Dawber, was installed in 1923 as a memorial to Walter Morrison of Malham Tarn House, benefactor of St Michael's.

Malham is only a mile north, either by road or the footpath past Scalegill Mill and its extensive array of millponds and canals. A mill has stood on this site since the eleventh century, being used in turn for processing corn, wool, flax and cotton. The centre of

Malham Tarn House, home of Walter Morrison, in the early twentieth century.

Malham village is dominated by the Buck Inn, rebuilt in 1874 by Walter Morrison. Morrison (1836-1921) was a successful businessman from a family which had made its fortune during the Napoleonic Wars. He was given the Malham Tarn estate on coming of age, and represented Skipton in parliament as a Liberal Unionist during 1886-92 and 1895-1900.

He was not, however, a keen party politician, and was far happier indulging his business and philanthropic interests, especially those relating to the north of England. His guests at Malham Tarn House, three miles north of Malham overlooking the tarn, included John Ruskin, who donated a mosaic (now disappeared) to the Buck Inn, Charles Darwin, John Stuart Mill and Charles Kingsley. Kingsley's *The Water-Babies* was inspired by the scenery of Malham Cove and Littondale. Morrison was buried at Kirkby Malham.

Also in Malham is the Listers Arms, a three bay, three storey rubblestone house with mullioned windows, now an inn. Over the doorway is an oval panel containing the letters RRA, the date 1723, and a form of wine glass. The brightly-coloured encaustic floor tiles in porch and hall were a late nineteenth or early twentieth century addition. The Lister family of Gisburn owned the Malham Tarn estate before the arrival of Walter Morrison, later known as the Millionaire of Malham Tarn.

To the west of Malham and Gargrave lie Ribblesdale and the great dome of Bowland, partly drained by the River Hodder, a tributary of the Ribble. Hodder and Ribble between them form the boundary of the West Riding in the area west of Clitheroe. The Leeds & Liverpool Canal runs south-west from Gargrave, passing within a couple of miles of an Edwin Lutyens house, Gledstone Hall, at West Marton. The hall, built for industrialist Sir Amos Nelson in 1925-7, replaced an earlier John Carr work, while the garden was the work of Lutyens and his mentor Gertrude Jekyll, then aged over eighty.

After Barnoldswick the canal heads south into Lancashire, and to the west Pendle Hill nudges the West Riding boundary upwards on the map, separating Craven from Bowland.

The rivers Hodder and Ribble meet near Great Mitton, three miles south-west of Clitheroe; the Hodder drains the Forest of Bowland, and near its head, to the east of the Bowland dome, is Slaidburn. The Court of the Forest of Bowland sat at Slaidburn, in what is now the Hark to Bounty Inn, still complete with courtroom. The church of St Andrew has a fine Jacobean rood screen and a three-decker eighteenth century pulpit; the box and family pews still stand undisturbed in their original Georgian arrangement.

The B6478 south of the village takes the driver back into the Ribble Valley, though after crossing the Hodder at Newton a by-road to the west offers the chance to see Browsholme Hall, only five miles distant. The original house was built in 1507 but a new red sandstone façade was added around 1605-10 by Thomas Holt, a Yorkshire carpenter and architect who worked on several Oxford University buildings in the early 1600s. The centre of the façade has Doric, Ionic and Corinthian columns standing one upon the other; these superimposed architectural orders were a French idea of the mid-sixteenth century which caught on in Northern England. Later alterations and additions include a drawing room by Jeffry Wyatville dating from 1805. Inside Browsholme, the hall is much as it was in 1807 and contains a rare mix of family heirlooms.

At Sawley, four miles north-east of Clitheroe, the Ribble Way path changes banks and passes close to Sawley Abbey, a Cistercian house founded by William de Percy in 1147. Sallay, its medieval name, was never large but it developed a reputation for scholarship and its prior, William of Rymyngton, was also chancellor of Oxford University in 1372-3. Sawley was suppressed in 1536, but briefly restored during the Northern rebellion known as the Pilgrimage of Grace, under Abbot William Trafford. The pilgrimage was rapidly crushed by the use of martial law, including public hangings; Trafford was executed on the 10th March 1537 and the abbey again suppressed.

Today the outlines of the abbey buildings may still be seen, with the church standing out most clearly. The gateway across the road just north of the church was built of material from the abbey site after excavations there in 1848. From Sawley Bridge a footpath runs two miles north to Bolton-by-Bowland, a pretty village with two greens and a small nineteenth century development of Jacobethan cottages which relate to nearby Bolton Hall.

The original hall dated from at least the fifteenth century, but was rebuilt in the Gothic style for John Bolton in 1806-8 by Joseph Gandy. Gandy, an eccentric architect and painter of architectural fantasies, also worked for Bolton at Storrs Hall near Windermere.

Rainsber Scar, the limestone cliff overlooking the Ribble to the south of Bolton Hall, is said to be the site of a spectacular escape by the hall's sixteenth century owner Sir William Pudsay. When discovered to be minting money from his own mine he fled on horseback over the cliff, somehow survived and was eventually pardoned.

The Ribble Way follows the beautiful Ribble Gorge closely in this area, taking the walker three miles upstream to the attractive but busy village of Gisburn. The handsome Ribblesdale Arms dates from 1635, but the delightful Gothick gate lodges of Gisburne Park are most memorable sight in Gisburn, guarding the southern entrance to the park with an ethereal mixture of pinnacles and points. The pair of lodges, really just intricately-decorated boxes, were designed by the owner of the park, Lord Ribblesdale, around 1800. Close to the lodges, castellated parapets mark the entrance of a railway tunnel dating from 1880, part of the old Lancashire & Yorkshire line connecting Clitheroe and Hellifield. Gisburne Park itself, now in institutional use, was built in 1727-36; later alterations include a circular double-height domed room added around 1800. The interior of the main house is decorated with elegant Baroque plasterwork.

The railway (and the A682) follow the Ribble Valley six miles north to Hellifield, which became a railway junction in 1880 with the extension of the Lancashire & Yorkshire line to meet the Midland Railway just outside the village on the edge of the moors. Pullman cars ran from Manchester to Scotland via Hellifield and the Settle & Carlisle line, and the village became a small railway town, but all this activity ceased some years ago. The Ribble Way bypasses Hellifield to the west but takes in Rathmell on its way north into Ribblesdale. North of Rathmell Church, built in 1842, is a row of cottages at right angles to the road. This is College Fold, where the first Nonconformist college was founded in 1670 by Richard Frankland, born in the village in 1630.

The Ribble Way rejoins the river nearly two miles south of Giggleswick and its near neighbour Settle. Giggleswick stands in the lee of Giggleswick Scar, and although best-known for its school and church, the village has several fine door datestones, some of the most decorative and distinctive in the Dales. The lintel is usually large and flat with a deeply-incised design, often using curving forms. The church of St Alkelda, an Anglo-Saxon saint said to have been martyred by the Danes, is largely fifteenth century with handsome seventeenth century furnishings. There is also a defaced monument to Sir Richard Tempest, who founded a chantry in the church; he was buried in 1488 with the head of his favourite horse beside him.

Giggleswick School, to the west of the village, was founded in 1553 but is now housed in a collection of grey stone buildings dating mainly from 1867-9 onwards. The school

An early view of Victoria Street, upper Settle.

chapel, south of the main campus, is outstanding, and its glorious green copper-covered dome can easily be seen from the hills across the valley. It was donated by Walter Morrison of Malham, who insisted the chapel should have a dome, an idea prompted by his fondness for Palestinian buildings. His architect was Sir Thomas Jackson, renowned for his 'Jacksonbethan' buildings in which he tried to create a style including both Gothic and Classical elements. Jackson had never before built a dome, and was keen to show that the combination of dome and Gothic was compatible; he designed the chapel in 1897 and it was completed in 1901. The dome is externally octagonal and internally a hemisphere. The chapel's interior is decorated with mosaics and coloured marbles.

Settle developed rapidly in the thirteenth century, acquiring a market in 1249 and serving Ribblesdale and Craven. The town's narrow streets and tiny courtyards still retain many good seventeenth century and Georgian buildings. The centre of the town is Market Square, where the town hall and Shambles may be found. The town hall was built (originally as public rooms) by George Webster in 1832 using a local version of the Jacobean style. The Shambles is seventeenth century below and late Victorian above; the space under the arches, once open, was used for the conduct of market business.

From behind the town hall, Cheapside leads to the High Street and the Folly, a seventeenth century house with wildly-exaggerated Gothic decoration on a basically Tudor form. The doorway is dated 1679 and has a fantastic surround, the columns appearing to have been squeezed near their tops. The house acquired its name because the builder, one Thomas Preston, ran out of money before he could complete his *tour de force*. Another Settle oddity is the Naked Man café, which bears on its wall a carving of a man holding a well-placed datestone reading 1663.

The A65 west of Settle runs below Giggleswick Scar up to Buck Haw Brow, then along the edge of the Wenning Valley towards

Clapham. Clapham is six miles from Giggleswick by road or eight minutes by train, though these are infrequent and both stations are a mile or so from the villages they serve. Best is the round trip, out on foot and back by rail, setting out from Giggleswick either towards Stackhouse along the Ribble Way (the footpath runs north along the west bank of the Ribble from Settle Bridge), or taking the path along Giggleswick Scar which leaves the A65 half a mile north-west of Giggleswick. From the scar the view takes in the lines of the Craven Fault. If at Stackhouse turn north-west, or from the scar go north above Buck Haw Brow, and the routes meet on the way to Feizor, where Hale Lane bridlepath goes on to Austwick. On the far side of the village, Thwaite Lane leads down through the grounds of Ingleborough Hall into Clapham. (The distance is between seven and eight miles, depending on the route followed.)

Thwaite Lane is part of the old packhorse route between Lancaster and Richmond; it literally passes through the Ingleborough Hall estate in two tunnels, dug to preserve an unsullied view for the Farrers, who built Ingleborough Hall around 1820-30. The Farrers have been associated with Clapham since the early eighteenth century, and erected their new home on the foundations of a former shooting lodge. It has an imposing Classical façade with pleasant curving bays, and the entrance hall displays pillars and a staircase of Dent marble, a polished greeny-grey limestone. A 200 yard long tunnel took servants between hall and village, and a fine ice-house was cut into the hill behind the hall. Between 1810 and 1830 the Farrers turned the

valley of Clapham Beck into a picturesque landscape garden by damming the beck to form the Lake, a half mile long extension of the original Clapham Tarn. Clapdale Drive was constructed to take visitors around the estate in their carriages, and the tunnels built to remove strollers along Thwaite Lane from sight. James Farrer provided electricty for Clapham in 1896 by using the waters of the lake to drive a turbine which powered a generator. His son Reginald John Farrer (1880-1920), an eminent botanist and traveller, introduced many hundreds of new species to Europe. He almost re-invented the rock garden, building a famous example at Ingleborough, and his enthusiasm for collecting eventually drove him to his death on an expedition to Burma. Parcevall Hall near Appletreewick also features plants collected by Farrer.

The village of Clapham is split in two by Clapham Beck, which is crossed by three stone bridges. The National Park Centre was originally the manor house and bears a datestone reading WCI 1701. It was the home of the Inglebys, who bought the manor from the Clapham family in the sixteenth century. The Claphams were given the manor by Henry II in the twelfth century, and lived at Clapdale Castle, which stood above the village near Clapdale Scars. The tower of St James Church dates from around the fifteenth century, but the remainder was completely rebuilt in 1814. The church is beautifully sited beside the beck, and just to the north is the entrance to Clapdale Drive, which takes the walker through Clapdale Wood and on to Ingleborough Cave. This spectacular cave reaches far into Ingleborough, past the 'Inverted

The church of St Leonard at Chapel-le-Dale.

*The Kempe window of 1898 at St Leonard,
Chapel-le-Dale.*

Batty Moss Viaduct at Ribblehead.

Forest' of stalactites in the direction of Gaping Gill, an alarming pothole.

The path past the cave leads on and up to the summit of Ingleborough, and an alternative descent passes through Ingleton via a bridlepath leading south-west from the summit. It was the arrival of the railway from Skipton in 1849 which turned Ingleton into a tourist centre, though its earlier history was industrial - coal-working followed by cotton and lime. The coal industry was revived in 1913 with the opening of Ingleton Colliery, but it closed in 1935.

Tiny Ingleton was once the proud home of two railway stations, one either side of the viaduct over the Greta. On the east side was Ingleton Station, owned by the North Western, while on the west was Thornton Station, owned by the London & North Western. When the Midland railway absorbed the little North Western, hostilities broke out over the viaduct, and passengers wishing to travel northwards through Ingleton had not only to to change trains but to walk across the viaduct! Now, however, the village has no station at all.

Ingleton Church, St Mary, was rebuilt (apart from its tower) in 1887, but contains a circular Norman font with sculptures showing the early life of the Virgin Mary. The church is the starting point for the Waterfalls or Ingleton Glens Walk, an almost compulsory (and therefore often crowded) classic walk past gorges, waterfalls and confusing geological strata. Into the Twiss Valley, on through Swilla Glen, and past Pecca Falls to Thornton Force, this is an unforgettable four miles.

Oddies Lane, an old Roman road up the Doe Valley from Ingleton, brings the traveller directly to the church of St Leonard at Chapel-le-Dale. This tiny, isolated church began life as a chapel of ease for St Mary at Ingleton, and probably dates from the fourteenth or fifteenth century. The stone slate roof is supported by four hefty wooden king-posts and tie beams; the bright interior has a beautifully-coloured window designed by Kempe & Co in 1898, east of the south door. The Kempe trademark, angel's wings in the form of peacock tail-feathers, are clear. The church was rebuilt in 1869, the same year in which work began two miles to the north-east on the Batty Moss Viaduct, the greatest of them all on the Settle & Carlisle railway line.

The Settle & Carlisle was a product of more railway rivalry, being constructed to give a through route to Scotland for the Midland Railway and enable it to compete with the LNER and LNWR London-Scotland lines. Midland general manager James Allport explored the prospective route on foot in the autumn of 1865, surveying began in 1869, and by July 1870 a hutted village for the navvies and their familes had been erected at Batty Green, the boggy area just east of the Batty Moss Viaduct at Ribblehead. The line, crossing seventy-two miles of impossibly difficult country, and with twenty-three viaducts and fifteen tunnels (including those on the Hawes branch), was opened in 1875. There were many deaths during construction, including those of women and children; a smallpox epidemic struck Batty Green in 1871. The dead are commemorated by a plaque, designed in the form of a castellated tunnel entrance, in Chapel-le-Dale Church.

North of Settle, the railway runs beside and sometimes across the Ribble until Ribblehead,

An aqueduct crosses the Settle-Carlisle Railway south of the Blea Moor Tunnel, near Ribblehead; Ingleborough is in the background.

The Dent Head Viaduct on the Settle-Carlisle railway.

where the pair diverge and the railway enters Blea Moor Tunnel, at 2,629 yards the longest on the line. The tunnel entrance is easily seen from a point one mile north of the Batty Moss Viaduct, where a monumental stone aqueduct carries a stream and a footpath over the line. The route of the tunnel is marked by a series of enormous air shafts dotted across the surface of Blea Moor. The railway emerges on the edge of Dentdale, immediately crossing

The Dent Head Viaduct.

The village of Dent and the church of St Andrew.

the Dent Head and Artengill viaducts before traversing another chunk of moorland and dropping into Garsdale.

Dent is the only settlement of any size in Dentdale, the valley of the Dee. Its narrow cobbled streets enclose the church of St Andrew, hidden behind whitewashed cottages; its churchyard looks out over the luxuriant green dale. Dent marble, used in the chancel, was produced from limestone

Looking east along Dentdale from the churchyard of St Andrew in Dent.

quarries higher in the valley. A huge slab of granite on the main street near the church is the memorial to pioneer geologist Adam Sedgwick (1785-1873), a local man who became professor of geology at Trinity College,

The granite memorial to Adam Sedgwick in Dent.

Cambridge. The Sedgwick family are also commemorated in stained glass inside the church.

An important village industry in the seventeenth and eighteenth centuries was hand-knitting. Local knitters produced mainly socks and gloves, and used large wooden hooks to support the knitting needles. Cottages were often equipped with spinning galleries, external first floor wooden balconies, which allowed spinners and weavers to work in good light.

At the foot of Dentdale the Dee meets the Rawthey; just upstream in the Rawthey Valley lies Sedbergh, nestling below the smooth, grassy hills of the Howgill Fells. Sedbergh has been a market town since 1251, and its busy Main Street is often awash with traffic. Near the west end of the town stands the church of St Andrew, partly Norman but largely thirteenth century, with a long and impressive clerestory.

To the south-east of the church is the library, which was built in 1716 and originally housed Sedbergh School. It is a delightful piece of idiosyncratic Classicism, quite out of keeping with the generality of local buildings. The renowned school was founded in 1525 by local man Roger Lupton, who became provost of Eton. It now occupies much of the valley south of the town. Several of its buildings, which are now mainly late Victorian and early twentieth century, were by the long-lived architectural practice Paley & Austin of Lancaster, including the sandstone chapel of 1897, south along Loftus Hill from the library.

At Brigflatts, a mile and a half south-west of Sedbergh via the Dales Way path alongside the Rawthey (or the A683), is a famous early

The Friends meeting house, Brigflatts.

Friends meeting house, dated 1675, white-walled and sparely furnished. It is a peaceful and secluded spot. The Rawthey forms the border with Westmorland west of Brigflatts, border and river running a mile or two south to the meeting of Rawthey and Lune. The border then retreats northwards along the Lune to Gibbet Hill, on the western edge of the Howgill Fells.

This hanging corner of the West Riding has one final surprise in store, the Waterside Railway Viaduct at Low Branthwaite, two

The Waterside Railway Viaduct.

miles north-west of Sedbergh. It stands half a mile north of the A684 crossing of the Lune, a footpath (part of the Dales Way) running north from the bridge on the east bank. It was built in 1861 for the London & North Western Railway by engineer John Errington; Errington and Joseph Locke were responsible for the Lancaster & Carlisle line, completed in 1846 and part of the first London-Scotland mainline route. The Waterside viaduct was part of the line connecting Low Gill, about three miles north, with Ingleton. The line is now closed, but the latticed iron central arch of the viaduct still rises arcade upon arcade 100 feet above the river, a fitting point to end an exploration of this most northerly extreme of the West Riding.

BEER, BURMANTOFTS
AND BRODRICK

Round and About Leeds

One of the best buildings in Leeds, and some would say the very best, is hidden away in Hunslet beside the obnoxious A61 almost two miles south of the city centre. On Whitfield Place (off Whitfield Way and Hunslet Road) stands the Garden Gate, a complete Edwardian drinking palace, a public house glittering and glowing with glorious colours in tiles and mosaics, with glasswork and joinery to match. There are plenty of buses from the centre of Leeds to this little haven, which represents the confidence and prosperity of the early twentieth century city just as the impossibly grand town hall epitomises the irrepressible spirit of mid-Victorian Leeds.

There has been a pub on the site of the Garden Gate since the 1820s, but the current pub dates from 1902 when it was rebuilt, possibly by local commercial architect Thomas Winn who was responsible for a handful of showy city pubs. The lower part of the façade is a fine advertisement for Burmantofts faience, the tough glazed ceramic material which could be produced in complex forms. Burmantofts was the tradename of the Leeds Fireclay Company, itself the result of an 1889 amalgamation of several Leeds ceramics companies. Colourful tiles and faience were manufactured at Burmantofts, just east of the city centre, from about 1880. Although the tile side of the business was closed in 1904, the Burmantofts works near Torre Road continued in production until 1957. Their wares were so popular that these souvenirs of Leeds can still be found in pubs and many more salubrious locations throughout Britain, though the works has been demolished.

The bronze-brown façade of the Garden Gate shines in the rain and glows in the evening sun, but the true delight is its interior. A curved yellow and green ceramic bar counter dominates the tap room on the left, with its floor-to-ceiling tiling and elegant Classical back bar-fitting. A tiled corridor gives access to the smoke room and lounges, all equally well furnished by Claughton of Hunslet. The lavish rebuilding of the Garden Gate signified a certainty that progress and prosperity would continue to befriend Leeds in the new century as they had, almost without a break, since the engine of industry began its surge forward around 1780.

Leeds was probably in existence as a settlement as early as the fifth century, and was a flourishing village at the time of the *Domesday* survey. In 1207 the Norman baron Maurice Paynel tried to prompt urban growth by giving the settlement a borough charter. This thirteenth century 'new town' was centred on the street now known as Briggate, which then, as now, leads to a river crossing, though the Aire was probably not bridged until 1384.

The new Leeds prospered. Not only did it stand at an important river crossing, but it was on the York-Chester road, near the Wharfedale route through the Pennines and close to the farming communities to the east. Expansion of the West Riding textile industry in the century after 1450 placed Leeds at the junction of thriving farming and industrial areas.

The Leeds textile industry was a mixture of general manufacturing, and finishing of cloth brought in from villages to the south and west. The main cloth market was located on and around Leeds Bridge, but was removed to Briggate in 1684 because of the pressure of crowds and the riverside fog. By the late seventeenth century the population of the extensive parish had risen to nine or ten thousand, but Leeds itself remained a compact settlement surrounded by gardens, orchards and other cultivated land. During the early to mid-eighteenth century the West Riding wool textile trade continued to grow and prosper,

and with it the status of Leeds as a general market centre. The cloth markets were held twice a week, attracting clothworkers and merchants who stayed to buy necessities from shops and stalls in Briggate and the Headrow, and found entertainment at the inns of Briggate. Many merchants also had town houses in Briggate, with finishing workshops attached. By 1800 Leeds had become a social centre for an élite of affluent merchants and professionals, who demanded nothing but the latest fashions in building and the arts.

The greatest period of industrial growth in Leeds began in 1780, when new sources of power were first harnessed in the textile industry. Leeds was well-placed in terms of transport and raw materials to benefit from technological advances. The Aire east of the town was made navigable by the work of the Aire & Calder Navigation, promoted by Leeds merchants and the corporation, between 1699 and 1704. The Leeds & Liverpool Canal was completed in 1816, and the railway arrived in 1834 in the shape of a line from Selby. The nineteenth century saw the rise of diverse enterprises such as mechanical engineering (often producing machinery for the textile industry), earthenware manufacture and a range of other concerns deriving from the basic needs of the population. Corn-milling and malting were foremost amongst these.

By the start of the twentieth century Leeds was regarded, at least by its own inhabitants, as the 'commercial metropolis of Yorkshire', and the success of its Victorian merchants and manufacturers is reflected in the buildings of the city centre, as is their taste in architectural style. The town hall in Victoria Square is the obvious and necessary place to begin an

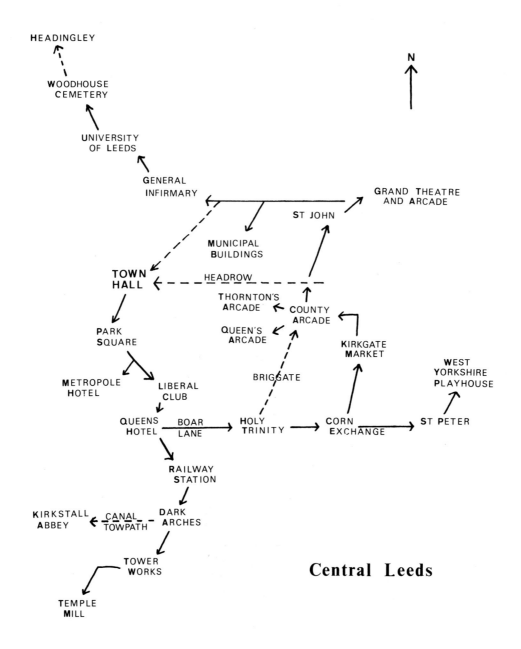

Central Leeds

exploration of this northern capital. It is solid, unmistakable, gargantuan and basks in an unshakeable security that the future will be as prosperous as the past. The design is Classical, a vast colonnaded box topped by a domed 225 foot high clock-tower.

The idea of a public hall was first mooted in 1850, a year after a company had been formed in neighbouring Bradford to build St Georges Hall. This hall was simply a large public space, and the idea of a similar, but of course larger, version for Leeds did not initially receive much support. The proposal was amended to include assorted municipal offices, and an open design competition was set in 1852. It was won by the young and almost unknown Cuthbert Brodrick of Hull, who had practised in his home town since returning from a tour of Europe in 1845. There he had fallen for French and Italian architecture, both Classical and contemporary, and the monumentality and style of the buildings he experienced abroad certainly influenced his own work.

His original town hall design placed the public hall at the centre of four corner pavilions, and the foundation stone was laid in 1853, two weeks before the opening of Bradford's St Georges Hall. The final design was under discussion as the building rose, and in 1856 Brodrick was instructed to add the tower, which dominates the whole composition. Queen Victoria opened the town hall in 1858; the streets were lined with palm trees and triumphal arches, 18,000 children sang the national anthem and the town became capital of the Empire for a day. The central hall, the Victoria Hall, was decorated in Classical style but incorporated Leeds symbolism; it alone was larger than St Georges Hall. Did the queen take heart from the abrupt Yorkshire sayings which also formed part of the hall's decoration: 'Honesty is the Best Policy', 'Weave Truth with Trust' and simply 'Forward'? Perhaps.

The town hall was built in millstone grit, which is tough to carve, thus the ornament is large-scale and fits well with the overall size of the building. The panel above the entrance, depicting the Leeds contribution to arts, science and industry, was carved in a softer stone by John Thomas, architectural protégé of Prince Albert. The four Portland stone lions guarding the steps on Victoria Square were Brodrick's final addition to the hall in 1867; he had been attracted to the idea by the sight of sculptured lions near public buildings when abroad.

Though many of the hall's interiors have been altered, the entrance hall has been restored using a colour scheme of 1895. The multicoloured encaustic floor tiles were by Minton & Co of Stoke on Trent, their Classical designs being typical of the style much used in mid to late Victorian public buildings.

From the town hall, cross Victoria Square and then Westgate, and walk south along Park Square East to find yourself transported back to Georgian Leeds in Park Square. Brodrick's dome looms above the only square to be completed in Leeds, begun in 1778 though not finished until 1794 and lacking a unified plan. It was part of the residential development of the West End which took place between 1760, when the Parks Estate was sold, and 1797. But by the turn of the century the wealthy were moving out of the centre, away from the warehouses of

The Liberal Club on Quebec Street.

Wellington Street which slowly spread north to engulf the West End.

Turning to the south side of the square, a most peculiar (and attractive) building faces the puzzled observer: St Pauls House. Its combination of extravagant Moorish-cum-Gothic decoration and substantial glazing suggests an outlandish department store, but it was in fact a warehouse and factory built in 1878 for industrialist Sir John Barran, the first wholesale mass producer of ready-made clothing. Its architect was Thomas Ambler (1838-1920), the son of a Leeds engineer who began his own architectural practice in 1860 and worked from Park Place, two streets south of Park Square, from 1867. He had the usual varied provincial commercial practice with one inspired exception, his work for Barran. Ambler designed several warehouses for Barran's firm, mainly in the 1870s.

The design of St Paul's House probably resulted from collaboration between Barran and Ambler. The warehouse was a relatively new type of building, first seen in the 1830s, and its ornamentation was still a problem for both architect and client. Status and respectability could be suggested by the use of Italian imagery, but the bright colours, use of terracotta and tiles, and Moorish forms of St Pauls House stem from the design of the great Islamic palace of the Alhambra in Granada. The terracotta and tiles of St Pauls House were manufactured by Doultons of Lambeth, but the minarets had to be replaced by convincing fibreglass copies during restoration in 1976.

The original ornate entrance of St Pauls House is sited on the corner of St Pauls Street, south of the square's centre. From the entrance, walk east along St Pauls Street, turn right into King Street then left into Quebec Street. Two brilliant pinky-red terracotta façades immediately stand out, the lush Metropole Hotel on King Street and the Liberal Club, with its

The sumptuous exterior of the Garden Gate public house in Hunslet.

striking round, open, corner tower, on Quebec Street. Both were designed by local architects Charles Chorley and John Connon, the Metropole in 1897-9 and the Liberal Club in 1890. Continue past the club to City Square.

Standing proud on the far side of the busy square is the massive grey-white form of the Queens Hotel, built for the London Midland & Scottish Railway and opened in 1937. It acts as the front for Leeds City Station, and was built as the final act in the railway wars of Leeds, which had resulted in the town having four separate stations by the 1860s, none in a truly central location.

Wellington Street Station then catered for five distinct railway companies, and the pressure this created was alleviated by the opening of the adjacent Leeds New Station

Terracotta detail on the façade of the Metropole Hotel, King Street.

(and original Queens Hotel) in 1869, the station being built on arches over the Aire. Its line to Marsh Lane Station, east of the centre and previously terminus for the line from Selby, clambered over the main streets of the town on a series of bridges and viaducts, then crossed the parish church burial ground on an embankment designed to avoid disturbance to the graves. Train whistles were banned as sacrilegious noise, and semaphore signals had to be used instead.

The railway companies, jealous of their autonomy, held out against a single central station until the threat of hotel development on the Headrow in 1933. This would have challenged the prime position of the Queens Hotel, and thus spurred on the railway companies to amalgamate their stations into the single Leeds City and build the new hotel. The architect officially responsible for the Queens was LMS chief architect William H Hamlyn, but his associate W Curtis Green was involved more directly. The 115 foot high Portland stone façade is in stripped Classical style with Art Deco touches, though contemporary advertising described it as 'cosmopolitan classic with a decided transatlantic base'. The interior was not only sumptuously decorated, but technically and even socially advanced: it was the first air-conditioned hotel in Europe, double glazing was provided and all 206 rooms had a bath.

Boar Lane leads east from the Queens Hotel side of City Square, connecting the Georgian and Victorian western part of the centre with the city's original centre around Briggate. Boar Lane itself was a fashionable residential street for wealthy merchants in the seventeenth and early eighteenth centuries, but commerce took over completely by the mid-nineteenth century. The south side exhibits a fine mix of buildings, including several by Ambler, who designed many of the stylistically very varied collection on Boar Lane in the 1870s.

Towards Briggate is Holy Trinity Church, built for the select inhabitants of the Boar Lane area in 1722-7. The idea of a church was mooted in 1714, but no funds were available until the formidable benefactor Lady Elizabeth Hastings came forward in 1722.

Apart from its spire, the church was designed by William Etty, architect and master carpenter of York. The interior is dominated by the giant Corinthian columns of the nave, though all is not what it seems: the height of the nave was increased by two feet in 1887 by the obvious expedient of lowering the column bases. No spire was originally intended, but it appears that this did not please the congregation, for a tiny one was soon added. It was replaced in 1839 by the most memorable feature of the exterior, a many-tiered square spire designed by Sir John Soane's pupil Robert D Chantrell, who practised in Leeds between 1819 and 1846.

Almost immediately east of Holy Trinity are the shops of Briggate; looking south towards Leeds Bridge the excellent late Victorian façade of Dysons survives amidst reconstruction and rebuilding. The present bridge, with its cast iron parapet, was designed by T D Steel and built in 1871-3. Cross Briggate and continue along Duncan Street to the Corn Exchange.

No visit to Leeds is complete without a sight of this outwardly rugged building, designed by Cuthbert Brodrick and built in 1861-3. It replaced the exchange constructed

The tower of Holy Trinity Church, Leeds.

in 1827-8 at the north end of Briggate, which had become too small for the corn merchants by 1860. Brodrick won the commission in competition and produced an elliptical plan, influenced by the circular corn exchange in Paris, for the tightly-constrained site.

Inside the Corn Exchange is a vast space ringed with offices, fifty-nine of them, on two floors. The light is unexpectedly bright, resulting from glazing in the domed ceiling which rises seventy-five feet above floor level. The off-centre glazing provided the clear northern light required by corn merchants for examining grain. The Corn Exchange has been restored to use as a shopping centre, and in consequence its interior has been altered to reveal the basement, but it remains a remarkable building.

Going north of the Corn Exchange, briefly up Call Lane then into Kirkgate, we find Kirkgate Market. A quarter mile east on Kirkgate is the parish church of Leeds, St Peter's.

It was built in 1837-41 to replace the much-altered medieval church which stood on the same site. When Walter Farquhar Hook became vicar of Leeds in 1837 he felt that his new church was inappropriate to combat the rising tide of dissent; its interior was a confusing amalgam of additions and alterations in which only the nave was used for services. He decided to rebuild, using R D Chantrell as his architect; their aim was to reproduce the best of Gothic design, using stone and slates from the fabric of the original church as well as new materials.

The church was consecrated in 1841; Florence Nightingale was at the service, as was George Washington Doane, the Bishop of New Jersey, who took home with him influential ideas on church architecture. St Peter's was an unusual design. Its tower stands on the north front and its interior is crowded with dark, heavy galleries of cast iron, plaster and oak. Hook built twenty-one churches during his incumbency and succeeded in retrieving the declining position of the Church of England in Leeds; he also turned Leeds into a High Church town in contrast to the evangelicism of Bradford.

South of St Peter's, across Crown Point Bridge over the Aire, is Clarence Dock, the proposed site of the exciting new Royal Armouries Museum, to be designed by Danish architect Henning Larsen and set to open in 1996.

A quarter mile north of St Peter's along Church Lane and Somerset Street is the West Yorkshire Playhouse, opened in 1990 after five years of planning and building. It is the work of the Edinburgh-based Appleton Partnership, who produced a two-colour brick edifice dominated by its monolithic fly-tower. Inside are two theatres and a shed-like restaurant-cum-bar with fine views over the city; the glazed dome of Brodrick's Corn Exchange stands out in the distance. The fly-tower is the theatre's saving grace, a piece of outright functionalism which sets the building apart from the run of modern barn-like supermarket-style structures.

The site was previously occupied by the Quarry Hill Flats, a vast estate erected in 1935-41 and consisting of long, high walls of flats laid out to a simple geometric ground plan. The estate was then the largest council housing project in England. It was a delight for architectural purists, with its elegant arched entrance, but the decline in popularity of the flats amongst their tenants made demolition inevitable; the end came in 1978.

On the high point of Quarry Hill now stands the monolithic Quarry House, completed in 1992 and the home of the National Health Service Management Executive and the Benefits Agency. This forbidding and blank-faced structure is set in public gardens and occupies one of the best sites in Leeds, if not the West Riding. It is sad that the public are not invited to view the city from within its lofty walls; an opportunity missed, but a reflection of the current state of public building.

The cathedral-like spaciousness of Kirkgate Market is best appreciated from the gallery (leading to the café) above the bustle of the ground floor market stalls. The market hall was built in 1902-4, replacing part of a cast iron and glass hall dating from 1857. The area had been used as a market since at least 1826-7, when the Free Market was laid out. This market sold cattle and pigs, fruit and vegetables, and hay and straw, and was the last of half a dozen market schemes to be carried out in prosperous 1820s Leeds. This commercial glut overloaded the market for markets, and not all the ventures succeeded. The Free Market flourished, however, becoming known as Kirkgate Market. By 1853 more covered market accommodation was needed, and the council allocated £14,000 for this purpose at Kirkgate. The borough surveyor's design, improved by Joseph Paxton of Crystal Palace fame, opened in May 1857. It was a Tudorised winter garden, lit by 200 gas lamps; the markets were rapidly leaving the streets.

Kirkgate Market.

Kirkgate Market was extended in 1875 and again in 1898-1900, after a fire in 1893 had severely damaged the building. The widening of Vicar Lane, the west frontage of the market, prompted the decision to rebuild once more, and work began on the present Kirkgate or City Markets in 1902. The architects were brothers John and Joseph Leeming of Halifax, known for their work on markets in Oldham and Halifax as well as their extension to the Admiralty Offices in London. The new market opened in 1904: its exterior resembles a monstrous Germanic town hall, while inside highly-decorative cast iron arcades focus on a central octagon. Iron dragons support the balconies, and a cast iron clock tower originally stood in the octagon. It now resides at the southern end of Roundhay Park, at the junction of Roundhay Road and Oakwood Lane.

To see another example of the glorious architecture thrown up by the turn of the century commercial development of Leeds, walk a little way north from Kirkgate Market along Vicar Lane to the entrance of County Arcade, on the left just after Queen Victoria Street. The arcade was built in 1898-1900 by Frank Matcham, theatre architect and designer of the Blackpool Tower Ballroom, and was part of a Leeds Estate Company development which included Matcham's Empire Palace theatre (1898) on Briggate, demolished in 1962.

The Estate Company bought up parcels of land between Briggate and Vicar Lane during the late 1890s and went ahead with their works in 1898. Shopping arcades had been introduced to Leeds twenty years earlier - indeed eight were built there by 1900 - and flourished where they connected established shopping streets or markets. County Arcade ran between the major shopping street of Briggate and the market area, and its palatial architecture contributed to its success. Matcham used local Burmantofts green and buff terracotta in mainly Classical forms, pink marble columns, mosaics and cast ironwork to produce an elegant and airy east-west route. Recent renovation has restored some hidden shopfronts and recreated others, long since gone missing. The overall effect is at first sight too theatrical, but what else would one expect from a Matcham design?

Emerging on to Briggate from County Arcade, the walker may continue onwards through Thornton's Arcade to the right or Queen's Arcade to the left. Thornton's was the first of the Leeds arcades, built in 1877-8 to a design by local architect George Smith for publican and entertainments magnate Charles Thornton. The arcade is tall, narrow and singularly Gothic, its roof glazing supported on iron horseshoe-shaped arches. This medievalism extended to the clock marking the Briggate entrance, which features mechanical figures from Sir Walter Scott's *Ivanhoe*, a dramatic tale involving King Richard I and Robin Hood. Queen's Arcade connected Briggate and the theatres beyond Lands Lane; it was a two-storey arcade, built in 1888-9 by architect George Clark of London.

From the north end of Briggate the walker may turn left to return to the town hall along the Headrow, a piece of city planning created in 1929-37, or cross to New Briggate to find yet another arcade and the oldest church in Leeds, St John.

St John the Evangelist stands on the west of New Briggate, though its entrance is in Mark Lane. It was built in 1631-4, during the reign of Charles I, and was given to the town by prosperous woollen merchant and renowned benefactor John Harrison. Externally it is unremarkable but the interior, with twin naves rather than nave and aisle, and a king-post roof, is unique. Best of all is the carved oak screen, resplendent with strapwork, dividing the naves from what at first sight should be the chancel. In fact the church was built without a chancel, according to the ideas of William Laud, Bishop of London; beyond the screen stood a communion table. There is much decorative wood and plaster work, all of which survived the Civil War but was almost lost in the early and mid-nineteenth century, when the architectural and liturgical taste of the clergy had completely changed.

Although pressure from architects Richard Norman Shaw and G G Scott averted complete demolition, the church was restored in 1866-8 by Shaw, when some woodwork and other detailing disappeared. During the 1880s and 1890s much of the old woodwork was found and reinstated, however, and today the interior presents a magnificent display of seventeenth century work by local craftsmen.

Almost opposite St John on New Briggate is the Grand Theatre, its turreted Romanesque façade instantly recognisable. It was built in 1876-8 by George Corson, a Dumfries-born architect who had moved to Leeds in 1849 to work with his brother, and taken over the practice around 1860. Corson's practice encompassed everything from houses and warehouses to a brewery (he was architect to Tetleys between 1864 and 1904) and a hospital, but the Grand was his only theatre; the design work was undertaken largely by his assistant James Robinson Watson, who had seen several foreign theatres at first hand.

Between them they produced a wonderful auditorium seating 2,600; it has three horseshoe-shaped balconies supported on iron columns, and rich decoration combining

Gothic and Classical motifs, even including fan vaulting. The local industrialists who put up the £62,000 required for the theatre must have been well pleased to hear it compared favourably with anything in America and perhaps France. Happily it is still in use and little has changed inside the auditorium, although the original stage machinery has been removed.

Beside the Grand on its north side is the Grand Arcade, built in 1896-8 by the New Briggate Arcade Company. The interior, originally twin arcades, is plain but sports a mechanical clock encouraging the passer-by to waste no time. Both street façades are faced with colourful Burmantofts ceramics. The late Victorian and Edwardian burst of arcade and market construction transformed shopping in Leeds, and helped to bring in wealth from outside the city.

The route back to the town hall leads left along Merrion Street from New Briggate, and continues along Great George Street. At Calverley Street, turn left to return to Victoria Square.

Across Calverley Street from the town hall are the municipal buildings, a vaguely Italianate pile by Corson, built in 1876-81 to provide the council with extra office accommodation. Now used as a museum and library, a glance into the entrance hall will reveal a sumptuous interior with colourful tiles, stone, mosaic and glasswork.

Next door is the unexciting art gallery, built in 1887-8 by Leeds architect William Thorp; Corson entered the architectural competition for this site, but his design was only placed third. Corson is best known for his city centre works, but one of his most memorable domestic commissions stands just off Otley Road at Weetwood, about three miles north-west of the centre. Here in 1875-7 he built Spenfield for banker James Walker Oxley, producing a Gothic-cum-Romanesque mansion full of colour and decorative delights.

Immediately east of the art gallery is the imposing dark granite façade of the Henry Moore Institute, designed in 1992 by London-based architects Ed Jones and Jeremy Dixon; it involved the conversion of three Victorian wool-merchants' houses on Cookridge Street.

North-west of the town hall on Great George Street stands the General Infirmary, built by George Gilbert Scott in 1863-7. It was the most advanced hospital of its day, planned on the pavilion principle advocated by Florence Nightingale and executed in polychromatic brick and carved stone. It replaced John Carr's 1770-1 infirmary which had become outdated and overcrowded by the 1860s. For the infirmary Scott chose the Gothic style, which he felt could combine function and beauty. He gave the infirmary's main south façade the same style of decoration as the Midland Grand Hotel at St Pancras Station in London, which he built in 1868-74. The infirmary lacks the towers of St Pancras but is still a surprisingly powerful building. It was originally symmetrical, but the most easterly pavilion was added, in the same style, by Corson in 1891-2.

Rounding the infirmary to east or west, one returns eventually to Calverley Street, which if followed away from the city centre and over the inner ring road will deposit the walker on the campus of the University of Leeds.

The campus boasts a happily eclectic mixture of buildings, the finest being the

Great Hall, built by Alfred Waterhouse for the then Yorkshire College in 1891-4. Towers, turrets and gables mark the skyline of its red-brick exterior, while the main staircase is faced in bright, coloured Burmantofts glazed ceramics. There are several parallels here with Waterhouse's series of Prudential Assurance offices. In 1904 the college achieved university status in its own right, and the square tower of the monumental neo-Classical Parkinson Building, completed in 1950, symbolises the progress of the institution from a group of twenty-four students in 1874.

On its northern margin the campus now incorporates the Woodhouse Cemetery on Woodhouse Lane, the town's first cemetery. It opened in 1835, and the entrance arch and chapel were designed by John Clark using the Greek revival style, which he brought from his native Edinburgh.

Just over a mile north-west is Headingley, the product of waves of suburbanisation spreading from the city centre. In 1801 the population of the Headingley area was only 300, but by 1834 many mansions and villas had been built there by the sucessful traders and manufacturers of Leeds. Good transport links with the centre encouraged the middle classes to move out to Headingley in the mid-nineteenth century, followed by the working classes in the 1880s. The wealthy moved a little further north to escape the crowds.

Headingley's church, St Michael, stands at the corner of Headingley Lane (the continuation of Woodhouse Lane) and St Michaels Road. It is the third church on the site, the previous versions, dating from 1626 and 1837, having proved too small for the prosperous and expanding suburb. It was built by John Loughborough Pearson in 1884-6. It has a tall tower and spire, and an interior which resembles a Gothic cathedral; Pearson was busy with his design for Truro Cathedral while St Michael's was under construction.

Another side of life is evoked less than a quarter mile north up the main Otley Road from St Michael's; here in Alma Cottages (fourth on the left after St Michael's Road) is a king among public conveniences, a castellated stone edifice fit for the residents of this street of Gothic semis. The whole development probably dates from the 1880s.

Some fine villas may be seen almost opposite Alma Cottages, by walking the block comprising Wood Lane, Grove Lane and Alma Road, whence one emerges on to the main road. There is towering yellow brick Whernside, Italianate Wheatfield Lodge, Gothic baronial Moorfield House and several more, most dating from the 1860s to 1880s. Despite alterations and later additions, this quiet backwater still gives the flavour of fashionable residential development in mid-Victorian Leeds.

Two miles farther along Otley Road in Adel is the church of St John the Baptist, a Norman gem tucked away in an obscure part of north Leeds. The wonderfully elaborate south doorway, with arch upon arch of carving, is unaltered, as is the bronze door-ring portraying a tiny man being swallowed by a monster. The church was probably built around 1140, and although the chancel arch was restored in 1878, the carvings on the capital heads are original, with a horizontal flying angel and a centaur amongst the motifs.

The journey from Adel to Pudsey takes in the western suburbs of Leeds, and can best be

Fulneck Terrace, overlooking the valley, in the mid-nineteenth century.

accomplished via the A6120 ring road, though Fulneck, our destination on Pudsey's southern edge, is almost on the route of the Leeds Country Way footpath. This path runs along Pudsey Beck south of the weavers' village of Fulneck, established in 1744 by the Moravians, members of a Protestant episcopal church which originated in Bohemia. A path beside the golf course leads up to the settlement.

The Moravians, who had gained converts amongst the West Riding weavers, governed their community according to a strict moral code, administered by elders at monthly meetings. Their communities became renowned for their industriousness and the emphasis placed on education. Village members received a small salary for their work, while profits went to the community as a whole.

Fulneck village in the early twentieth century.

The Moravian villages were among the most economically successful of all the alternative communities which sprung up in the eighteenth and nineteenth centuries.

At Fulneck, the first of seven Moravian villages built from 1744 to the 1780s in England and Ireland, a church, schools and houses were erected in a single row known as the Terrace. The Terrace was begun in 1746 and was originally a collection of separate buildings designed in a plain Classical style; they were connected between the 1780s and the early nineteenth century when extra stone-built school buildings were added. The total length of the Terrace is now over 250 yards. The Moravian legacy at Fulneck, where the Terrace overlooks the valley, is an oasis of calm on the edge of the city.

Temple Mill offices, Marshall Street.

The next port of call on the underbelly of Leeds is Beeston, most easily reached from Fulneck by returning to the ring road and heading east; after about five miles take the A653 back into Leeds. This is Dewsbury Road, marking the southern edge of Beeston, and just over a mile northwards stands the New Inn, on the right opposite Stratford Street. It is a grand example of Edwardian pub architecture and the use of ceramics. Its entire façade, including the two jolly oriel windows, is covered in glistening, coloured faience, the glazed ceramic material which came to prominence in the late Victorian period because of its hardwearing qualities.

Following Stratford Street west, then Tempest Road and Cemetery Road north, will take you across the motorway and into Holbeck, at the turn of the century an area of industry, and back-to-back and tightly-packed terrace houses. Many houses have been swept away by clearance schemes, some being demolished as early as 1898. Continue up Top Moor Side, passing the Britannia (designed by Thomas Winn in 1898) and Spotted Cow public houses, into St Matthews Street, turning right at the Kings Arms into Ninevah Road. Another quarter mile brings you to Marshall Street and the incomparable Temple Mill, an Egyptian temple persuaded into the service of Yorkshire industry.

Marshall Street was named after John Marshall (1765-1845), one of the great Leeds industrialists of the early nineteenth century. He began as a flax spinner in Adel, where he developed improved spinning machinery with engineer Matthew Murray, and then invested in massive new flax mills at Holbeck from 1792. His contribution was crucial to the success of the flax industry in Leeds, which at its peak in the 1850s employed 9,500 people. Along the west side of Marshall Street he built a series of factories, including a warehouse dating from 1806 at the north end of the street and Temple Mill itself, erected in 1838-41 at the height of the firm's prosperity.

Temple Mill was an advanced piece of single-storey construction, top lit by sixty-six conical glass domes and with a flat roof insulated by layers of plaster, tar and soil. The soil was seeded with grass to keep it in place,

Detail of a column capital at Temple Mill.

and sheep grazed upon the roof. The mill became legendary, appearing in Disraeli's novel *Sybil*, published in 1845, which portrayed the two nations of England, the rich and the poor. In its fictional form the mill was the factory built by Trafford, a good employer: 'one of the marvels of the district, one might almost say, of the country'.

The real Temple Mill was designed by Leeds engineer James Combe but its Egyptian façade was by Joseph Bonomi, Egyptologist and occasional amateur architect. Bonomi's father Joseph and brother Ignatius were both renowned architects, but the younger Joseph probably became involved with the Marshalls through his work as a sculptor in Yorkshire during 1835-6. In the mid-nineteenth century the Egyptian Revival style was normally used only for monumental structures in cemeteries or masonic halls, but perhaps the connection between Egypt and flax, or even the attraction of a monumentally impressive factory, persuaded John Marshall - or indeed his son James, by then running the firm - that their mill should have an Egyptian look. Even the beam engine powering the mill was given Egyptian-style ironwork.

More overwhelming still is the office block attached to Temple Mill, which was designed by Joseph Bonomi to resemble part of the

The Dark Arches, supporting Leeds City Station.

Temple of Horus at Edfu in Egypt, complete
with six huge columns topped by flowered
capitals. It is like no other office block in the
world. Joseph travelled widely in Egypt,
designing the Temple Mill offices between
trips in 1842-3. Perhaps the success of the
Egyptian-style mill persuaded the Marshalls
to let Bonomi have free rein to produce this
office-as-temple.

At the top of Marshall Street, turn right and
take the second left down to the Leeds &
Liverpool Canal towpath. Across to the north
are the long-inaccessible Dark Arches which
carry the railway station above the Aire. A
glimpse of this grim complex can be seen
from the towpath, but to investigate further,
cross the canal via bridge or lock and head for
Granary Wharf (off Neville Street), a shopping
complex inserted into the vast and gloomy
arches beneath the station. Although the
shopfronts have brought colour to this
powerful and eerie space, the Aire still exhibits
brute strength as it races through the long,
arched tunnels under the feet of shoppers.

Back on the towpath, two Italianate
chimneys stand out above the south bank;
they mark the Tower Works of pin manufacturer Thomas Harding, once Mayor of
Leeds and patron of the city art gallery. Leeds
architect Thomas Shaw designed the smaller
and more slender of the two chimneys in
1864, copying the Lamberti Tower of Verona
at the behest of Harding for the dust-extraction
chimney. The Italianate style had been popular
for factory chimneys since about 1850; they
were aesthetically pleasing, engendered good
publicity and had overtones of the power
games of Italian family politics. The second
chimney, built in 1899, is based on Giotto's

The Giotto Tower of Tower Works

The County Arcade, built at the turn of the century.

The tower of Leeds Town Hall.

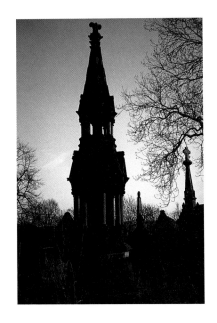

The Galli memorial in Beckett Street Cemetery.

campanile at Florence and constructed of a pleasing pinky-red brick with terracotta decoration.

The canal towpath may be walked westward, and forms the basis of the Museum of Leeds Trail, packed with industrial monuments but also passing near Kirkstall Abbey. From the Tower Works in a mile and a half the walker passes Armley Mill, built in 1804-5 by woollen manufacturer Benjamin Gott.

For Kirkstall Abbey, walk the same distance again and leave the towpath at Broad Lane. Cross colourful Kirkstall Bridge and go north along busy Abbey Road (A65); the magnificent Cistercian abbey, part of the crossing tower still standing almost to its original height, is soon visible.

The monastic community was first established in 1147 at Barnoldswick on land given by the Earl of Lincoln, but this proved unproductive and the colony moved on to the Kirkstall site, donated by one of the earl's vassals, in 1152. The abbey was largely built between 1152 and 1182, and the monks initially prospered through selling wool from their flocks. Later economic difficulties reduced the number of monks from about 36 to only 17, but at its dissolution in 1540 the number had risen again to 31. Although stone from the abbey was used in local building works, most of the major structures were left intact, and by the early eighteenth century Kirkstall was a well-known romantic ruin. Later repairs have ensured preservation, and the sheer bulk of the remaining buildings enables visitors to envisage the site in monastic use.

Returning to the canal towpath, in the next mile or so to the west the walker will pass the pretty Forge Locks and the three-rise Newlay Locks, where a path leaves the canal to the north-west heading for Newlay Bridge, one of the oldest iron bridges in the country. This elegant toll bridge over the Aire was built in 1819 with iron cast at the Shelf Iron Works, south-west of Bradford. John Pollard of Newlay House erected the bridge and his tolls were collected in the cottage at its north end.

Aficionados of public baths will find a fine example a mile south of Newlay Bridge. Head south along Pollard Lane, crossing Bradford Road into Newlay Lane, then right into Broad Lane. Across a road junction and on the corner of Calverley Lane is Bramley Baths, built in 1904 as part of a five year bath-building programme in Leeds. Splendid Edwardian decorative features remain on this newly-restored baths.

The canal towpath continues west as the valley broadens towards Bradford, but there is yet more to see in Leeds: travelling north-east from the centre on the A58 Roundhay Road, cross the junction with Harehills Lane and take the next left along Gledhow Valley Road. The road glides above woodland towards Gledhow Hall, attributed to John Carr and built around 1766-7. Its great delight is not Carr's architecture but a much later alteration, a splendid Burmantofts bathroom added in 1885; apart from the bath, almost everything was covered in ceramics, including the ceiling. The colours are mainly blue, brown and white, and though the marble-topped bath has disappeared, those lucky enough to see this example of Victorian cleanliness will doubtless imagine the virtue to be gained from bathing in such surroundings.

Alternatively, a right turn at the Harehills Lane junction, then right again into Ashley Road after half a mile, will bring the traveller to the edge of Burmantofts and the Beckett Street Cemetery. It was opened by the council in 1845 and boasts many well-crafted small sandstone monuments, as well as a polychromatic Gothic column dating from the 1880s in memory of numerous members of the Galli family. The Galli memorial is near the northern extremity of this peaceful cemetery.

If strolling back towards the city centre along Beckett Street, look out for the elegant new extension to the Agnes Stewart High School on Rider Street, just before the dual carriageway. Architects Abbey Hanson Rowe have produced an airy and unusual building from a mix of pastel blockwork and glass bricks.

But onwards to Roundhay Park, the prestigious suburb centred on Roundhay Park. The park entrance is at the top of Roundhay Road, past the old Kirkgate Market clock, but look out for the cool thirties Oakwood Fish Bar on the corner.

The ancient deer park of Roundhay was bought in 1803 by London banker Thomas Nicholson and Sedbergh businessman Samuel Elam. Nicholson died in 1821 and his brother landscaped the Nicholson share of the park in the 1820s; Elam's land was sold off as building plots for grand villas. The Nicholson family sold out to the corporation in 1872, after much debate as to the possible effects of public access on the park and its surroundings. The park proved immediately popular on its opening by Prince Arthur in September 1872, and its sham castle, castellated lodge and

temple can still be seen. The temple is in fact a drinking fountain presented by John Barran and designed by Ambler in 1882.

A journey of seven miles from Roundhay, via the ring road and the A63, will take the traveller to the great country house of Temple Newsam, idyllically situated on the eastern edge of Leeds (just a two mile walk from Cross Gates Station).

Before turning south for the house, a mile detour further back towards Leeds along the A63 to Halton will be rewarded by the sight of a massive and modern Gothic church, St Wilfrid, built by Arts and Crafts architect Randall Wells on Halton Hill in 1937-9. The exterior combines narrow pointed lancets and great square voids in the fenestration, but all is dominated by the gabled wooden spire. Inside, the woodwork was designed by Wells, who had previously worked for E S Prior and William Lethaby, two of the great names in Arts and Crafts architecture. A surprise indeed to find this piece of modern thinking (which sadly led nowhere in terms of church design) looming above a suburban council estate.

Temple Newsam House is a vast brick palace built by London financier Sir Arthur Ingram in the 1620s and 1630s on the site of an earlier house. Buildings on the estate were mentioned in the *Domesday* survey, but the original courtyard house was begun by Thomas, Lord Darcy between 1488 and Darcy's execution in 1537, a punishment for his part in the Pilgrimage of Grace.

Ingram bought Temple Newsam in 1622 and immediately set about rebuilding, using the traditional Elizabethan style rather than the fancy Italian ideas already abroad in London. Along the balustrade runs a homily in giant letters on the theme of glory to god and king. Generations of Ingrams made little impact on Temple Newsam until 1736 when Henry, seventh Viscount Irwin, inherited the property. He modernised much of the interior, but at such cost that he gave up the estate in 1758 in favour of his nephew Charles, who had made a good marriage. 'Capability' Brown was commissioned to update the park in 1762, and alterations to the house continued from 1768 until 1796 when the cupola was added. The nineteenth and early twentieth centuries saw more redecoration than rebuilding, though central heating was installed in the 1890s.

The house was bought by the city of Leeds in 1922, and almost all the contents were dispersed in a seven day sale. Temple Newsam is now a museum but its excellent interiors are slowly being restored, and in its park and seven gardens the visitor may taste the joys of country house life. Strangely Sir Arthur Ingram spent little time at Temple Newsam, preferring his York house; once the plaything of the rich, Temple Newsam now richly entertains us all.

WORSTEDOPOLIS

Bradford Dale

From the broad promenade running across Undercliffe Cemetery, both panorama and microcosm of Bradford can be seen: Bradford in its dale lies to the south and west, while nearby stand monuments to the great men of the city, the Victorian magnates of the cloth industry.

The cemetery, on Undercliffe Lane (off the A658 Otley Road about half a mile north-east of the city centre), was established in 1854, when Bradford was in the midst of its greatest period of growth. The Bradford Cemetery Company hired William Gay to landscape the site, and he combined steep, winding paths with the long promenade to great effect. Obelisks and pinnacles protrude from the promenade, while sphinxes guard an Egyptian-style mausoleum, dedicated to the Illingworth family. The memorial to textile millionaire Jacob Behrens is a massive Baroque tablet. This fine necropolis, itself a monument to the Victorian attitude to death, is a by-product of Bradford's mid-nineteenth century woollen boom.

Bradford Dale, the huge basin formed by Bradford Beck and its tributaries to the south of the Aire, was occupied by man as long ago as the Neolithic age. The *Domesday* survey shows that the area was inhabited in the late eleventh century, and by the mid-thirteenth century Bradford had become a market centre. Local woodlands and cloth-making were commercially important, and coal was being quarried from shallow pits by the fourteenth century. Population growth in the damp dale was slow, but by the mid-sixteenth century the cloth industry had assumed more than local significance. Cloth-making was a cottage industry, and villages in the western part of Bradford Dale began to specialise in the fine woollen cloth known as worsted. By 1773 the cloth trade in Bradford had grown sufficiently to warrant the erection of a piece hall, where pieces of cloth were bought and sold; it was sited at Piece Hall Yard, off Kirkgate.

The opening of the Bradford branch of the Leeds & Liverpool Canal in 1774 transformed the town's relations with the outside world.

Undercliffe Cemetery.

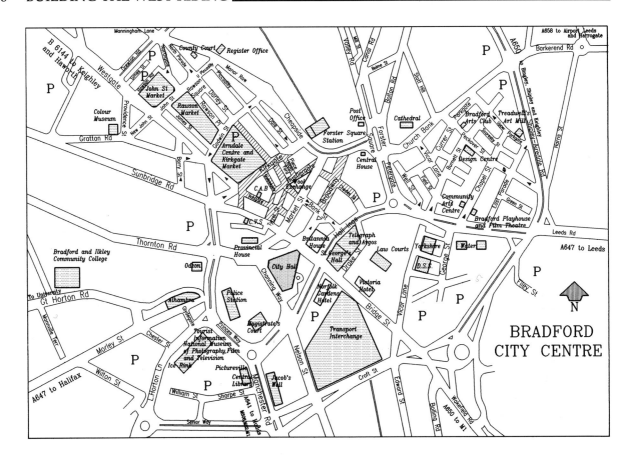

BRADFORD
CITY CENTRE

The memorial to architect William Mawson in Undercliffe Cemetery.

Riding's worsted output. Further mills, sited near water supplies, rapidly followed and mill-based textile manufacture eventually replaced home-based cloth making.

Coalmine workings spread throughout Bradford Dale during the seventeenth and eighteenth centuries, and by 1866 the annual production of Bradford's forty-six collieries was nearly two million tons. In addition, locally-available coking coal and ironstone made Bradford a major iron manufacturing centre in the nineteenth century. Coal contributed to the success of the cloth industry through steam-powered mills; technical innovations, for example power looms, increased the throughput of wool, which had reached over £23 million a year in the town by 1853. The textile warehouses were generally concentrated on the valley floor around the canal and later the rail heads; Bradford was connected to the national rail network in 1846.

By 1871 Bradford could boast 133 cloth mills, and the prosperity of the town has continued to rest largely upon its textile trade until the present time. Where better, then, to begin an exploration of Bradford than Little Germany, the tightly-packed area of palatial textile warehouses immediately to the south of the cathedral, between Church Bank and Leeds Road.

Visiting north German textile merchants first began to settle in Bradford in the 1830s, and the German trade in wool and yarns soon became vitally important to the town. Merchants of German origin made up about a quarter of the members of the Bradford Chamber of Commerce between the 1850s and the 1870s, and apart from their monuments in Undercliffe Cemetery, their greatest

The three mile link had ten locks, rising just over eighty-six feet from the junction with the main canal at Shipley, and a basin at Hoppy Bridge, near the present Forster Square. Holme Mill, one of Bradford's earliest textile mills, was built in the centre of the town, near Bradford Beck, in 1802, and by 1810 Bradford was producing about a quarter of the West

Warehouses in Little Germany.

memorials are the towering warehouses of Little Germany.

The earliest textile warehouses were built in the 1830s to the west of the canal basin in the Greek Revival style, and others of that era were strictly functional, lacking decoration or any attempt at sophisticated architectural styles. As the textile trade increased in importance, the face of its buildings changed: warehouses of the 1840s and 1850s began to imitate the palaces of late fourteenth century Florentine wool merchants. Bradford on the Aire, like Florence on the Arno, could parade its wealth. Much of Little Germany was built during 1860-73, when the textile trade was at its height, and even a brief stroll from Leeds Road into Well Street and Currer Street, and back via Vicar Lane, will give a glimpse of the interplay between power, wealth and architectural style which produced these warehouse palaces.

The typical warehouse was built roughly to a rectangular plan. The height was often five or six storeys, and as the streets of Little Germany are narrow, the effect is over-whelming. Stone exteriors were highly decorated in the Italianate or occasionally Gothic styles, while the staircase hall, usually placed on a canted (cut-off) corner, was often circular or octagonal and equally richly endowed. Prospective buyers were intended to be impressed as they climbed the stairs to first floor showrooms; the cloth itself arrived through large rear entrances, whence it could be hoisted to the top floor.

Warehouses on Vicar Lane include Law Russell (1873-4) and the American and Chinese Export (1871), both by Lockwood and Mawson of Bradford, and Briggs Priestley,

A view of Bradford in 1869.

with its massive yard gateway. The Briggs Priestley warehouse was built in 1866-7 by the local firm of Eli Milnes and Charles France, who made the greatest contribution to this palatial area of Bradford.

Across Church Bank from Little Germany stands the cathedral of St Peter. It occupies the site of a Norman church, but the present building dates from the fourteenth to sixteenth centuries, and was accorded cathedral status in 1919. Low in height, and with additions dating from 1899 to 1963, the exterior is unspectacular, but inside is a spired Gothic font cover, all Perpendicular tracery, and good stained glass of 1862 in the original chancel. The glass is by designers from Morris, Marshall, Faulkner & Co (which became Morris & Co in 1875), including Dante Gabriel Rossetti and architect Philip Webb.

The centre of Bradford is not inspiring: busy dual carriageways block the path at every turn, and too much new development is completely forgettable. However, before

Stone 'furniture' in Chapel Street, Little Germany.

escaping to the outskirts, which hold real interest, there are a few buildings worth a second glance.

Just west of the cathedral across Forster Square is a fine domed edifice: this is the Midland Hotel, erected by the Midland Railway around 1890 to front their newly rebuilt Midland Station (replaced by the modern Forster Square Station). Bradford's railway history is complex, involving several distinct companies, two main passenger stations and three goods stations. The resulting mess of railway tracks helped define the town's pattern of development. The Midland Hotel is currently disused, but the brilliant Burmantofts tiling in the entrance hall is just visible behind hoardings. Designer of both hotel and station was Charles Trubshaw, chief architect for the Derby-based Midland Railway.

The Wool Exchange is south of Forster Square, across Cheapside and about two hundred yards along Market Street on its west side. This glory of Worstedopolis has origins more Venetian than Florentine, with its arcaded Gothic façade and monumental tower. By the 1860s the cloth trade had outgrown the old piece hall, and the town's manufacturers and merchants prevailed upon John Ruskin to advise them on the most appropriate style for their new wool exchange. Ruskin devoted most of his Bradford lecture of the 23rd April 1864 to comments on the origins of architectural style, frustrating his audience who simply wanted the best wool exchange that £30,000 could build, but were unsure exactly how it might look.

They settled the matter with a competition, which caused endless acrimony as the winning design was both expensive and apparently inefficient, but leading local practice Henry Lockwood and William Mawson's colourful, decorative building was popular with the committee charged with taking the decision. The foundation stone of the towered Gothic Wool Exchange was laid by the prime minister in 1864 and the building opened in 1867.

Walking a little further along Market Street brings the best of Bradford's central buildings into view, the town hall, opened in 1873. Again won in competition by Lockwood and Mawson (using the pseudonym 'Let Bradford Flourish'), the town hall was another Gothic reminder of Italy, with a splendid 200 foot high tower based on that of the Palazzo Vecchio, the 'town hall' of Florence.

The cost was £100,000 and its opening was marked by a three mile long procession of the town's tradespeople; the outside world may have thought this a vulgar display, but for Bradford the building represented a reply to Leeds Town Hall (opened in 1858) and emphasised the growing status of their town. The 1905 extension was designed by the city architect with Richard Norman Shaw as consultant.

South of the town (now city) hall on Bridge Street stands the Metro Travel Interchange, for many their first sight of Bradford. Its vast glazed roof was built in 1973-7 to a design by architects from British Rail and the city council; under its translucent canopy, buses and coaches ferry passengers in relative comfort, and a bus maintenance depot hides beneath the main level. The £16 million bus station has spectacular good looks, especially after dark, but access from Bridge Street to both buses

The glazed bus station roof of the Metro Travel Interchange.

and trains, at the neighbouring Interchange, is not well thought out.

West of the town hall, only a couple of hundred yards away but across the inevitable dual carriageway, is the gleaming silver dome of the Alhambra Theatre, on its triangular corner site between Great Horton Road and Morley Street. The entrance is beneath the dome, which is carried on a drum of giant Corinthian columns. The theatre opened in 1914 and recent restoration has added a glazed foyer; the interior, with two balconies, has rich but restrained plasterwork.

Next door, two more domes signal entertainment in the form of the Odeon Cinema, originally the New Victoria Theatre, opened as a cinema-cum-theatre in 1930 and designed by Bradford architect William Illingworth. In contrast to the dazzling ceramic façades of some interwar Odeons, this cinema, built for Provincial Cinematograph Theatres, is in neo-Classical style with a mainly brick façade. Its seating capacity was 3,318, a tribute to the popularity of cinema in the 1930s. Today it functions as a two-screen cinema.

To escape from the city centre, follow Princes Way north into Godwin Street, turn left into Westgate and in a quarter of a mile right into Lumb Lane and Manningham, where essential Bradford begins. Here are massive textile mills and towering campanile chimneys expressing the architectural power of function and repetition.

In Lumb Lane, Lockwood and Mawson's Lumb Lane Mill of 1858-9 exhibits a finely-decorated chimney. The style of the mill was Italianate but the chimney was a more traditional octagonal section. The tall mill chimneys were necessary to provide strong draughts for steam-powered boilers, and were often built in the form of campaniles, separate but close to the parent mills, so that their immense foundations could be constructed more easily.

Cross via Grosvenor Road into Manningham Lane for a glimpse of suburban villa-dom in the latter part of the nineteenth century. In the early 1840s Bradford and Manningham were divided by green fields, woods and pleasant paths, but from 1845 the middle classes of Bradford began to invade Manningham Lane, with terraces in Eldon Place (1845), followed by Hanover Square and then Mornington Villas, built in 1852-74. A quarter mile north along Manningham Lane, turn left into Oak Lane; a further quarter mile will bring the explorer face to face with the vast Manningham Mill. Its Heaton Road façade stretches for over 350 yards and its magnificent campanile chimney is 249 feet high. The main part of the mill was built for Samuel Cunliffe Lister by local architects T G Andrews and Joseph Pepper in 1871-3. This Italianate monster mill had a floor area of sixteen acres, and the ornate chimney was modelled on the Venetian campanile in the Piazza San Marco.

Apocryphal tales abound regarding the celebrations which took place on completion of the chimney in 1873; one of the most amusing suggests that the entire board of Lister & Co were entertained to dinner in a room at the top of the stack.

Manningham Mill was built on land owned by the Lister family since the Middle Ages, and the chimney came to be seen as a symbol of Bradford's gentry, as opposed to the 'new money' of many millowners. The mill was the scene of a famous industrial dispute in the winter of 1890-1. Lister's mills then employed around 5,000 workers, many of them women, manufacturing silk velvets and plushes. In December 1890, Lister & Co informed its workers of an impending reduction in pay rates, due to increased competition and American protectionism. Although few workers were then trade union members, a strike involving almost the entire workforce ensued, which lasted nearly nineteen weeks through a harsh winter before its collapse. The end result was an increase in trade union membership throughout the West Riding textile industry.

Victor Road leads east from Manningham Mill to Lister Park, donated by the millowner to the people of Bradford in 1870. In the centre of the park, high above Keighley Road, stands Cartwright Hall, a monumental if eccentric pile in Edwardian Baroque which is the city art gallery. It originated with the donation of £40,000 by Samuel Lister to the town to replace the old Lister family home in the park. Lister suggested commemorating the inventor of the powerloom, Edmund Cartwright, but the council were given a free hand as to the nature of the building. They decided on a museum, not of technology but devoted to the socially more acceptable subjects of art and natural history. The architect, chosen by competition, was Sir John Simpson of London; the hall was built between 1900 and 1904, and its interior is full of dramatic spaces generated by colonnaded screens and arches.

At the north-east corner of the park stands a castellated gatehouse dating from 1883, and behind it a diminutive Albert Memorial-style structure erected in 1874 and dedicated to alpaca magnate and philanthropist Sir Titus Salt; its architects were Lockwood and Mawson. Salt was the father of the model village of Saltaire, two miles to the north in the Aire Valley.

The best introduction to Saltaire is reserved for walkers, who can leave the train at Shipley and follow the Leeds & Liverpool Canal towpath a mile west to Saltaire. (Take Briggate, the main Leeds road, a little way to Dock Lane, which leads to the canal basin.)

Here the Bradford Canal, which closed in 1922, joined the Leeds & Liverpool. Beside Dock Lane are the sad remains of canalside warehouses, their wharves suspended above the infilled course of the old canal. The route passes the sedate, Classically-designed Victoria Mill to the north of the canal and numerous small warehouses, whetting the appetite for Salt's monumental works.

Entering Saltaire along the canal towpath, the walker comes upon Salt's vast T-shaped Saltaire Mill stretching away from the south bank of the canal, balanced by his New Mill (1868) on the north bank, an Italianate pile with campanile chimney squeezed in between canal and River Aire.

Titus Salt (1805-76) made his fortune from alpaca wool, which was introduced into the textile industry from about 1830. Salt became mayor of Bradford, and by 1850 had decided to move his mill operation away from the overcrowded and squalid town into the country. He envisaged a community centred on the mill, with workers' housing of a high standard, and opportunities for education and healthy recreation. There were to be no public houses, however: 'Drink and lust are at the bottom of it all' summed up his feelings on the matter.

Bradford Wool Exchange,
soon after its opening
in 1867.

The Alhambra Theatre, Bradford.

*Approaching Salt's New Mill on the Leeds &
Liverpool Canal towpath at Saltaire.*

Salt first consulted architects Lockwood and Mawson about the new mill in November 1850, and later suggested buying part of the Crystal Palace for use as a weaving shed after the closure of the Great Exhibition. Sadly (one now feels) the architects dissuaded him, and proffered their own design which was built in 1851-3. The two-acre mill, engineered by Sir William Fairbairn, is six storeys high and has a south façade 545 feet long. The style is Italianate, with walls of local stone, two striking open towers on the south front and an ornate 250 foot high campanile (which has lost its decorative parapet). A second chimney, a copy of the Santa Gloriosa campanile in Venice, was added in 1868. Salt's mill, which could turn out eighteen miles of alpaca cloth daily by the late 1850s, was the first of the Italianate mills, and the style was taken up by many manufacturers.

The 895 houses of Saltaire village were largely complete by the mid-1860s. In keeping with the mill, they were all mildly Italianate in style, and were laid out on a grid pattern. The slope of the ground and the view of the moors to the north gave the village a picturesque feel. Salt provided a splendid Congregational church at the lower end of George Street. The Renaissance-inspired design with a semi-circular portico and domed tower was built in 1858-9 by Lockwood and Mawson. The Salt family mausoleum stands beside the church. Although Salt was an ardent Congregationalist, he gave several sites in the village for the construction of churches of other faiths.

After religion came provision for education; Saltaire School opened in 1868 and its institute in 1869, both designed by the village architects. The institute, the size of a small town hall and

Victoria Mill, Shipley.

The Congregational church in Saltaire, paid for by Titus Salt.

Germanic in appearance, accommodated all manner of recreational and educational pursuits, from reading and exercise to art and science. Outdoor recreation was catered for in the park, stretching along the Aire to the west of the mill and laid out by William Gay, who designed Undercliffe Cemetery. The park was formally opened in July 1871, and its serpentine walks still make for a pleasant stroll.

The velvet chains of paternalism may be escaped by taking the canal towpath west through the village, and either continuing on the towpath towards Bingley or heading north at the first lock after Saltaire Mill. The latter route crosses a bridge over the Aire and eventually enters Shipley Glen, after detouring around the houses of Glenwood Avenue.

The glen, a steep wooded valley, has been used as a pleasure ground by Bradford's inhabitants since at least Victorian times, and still retains its tramway, the Glen Railway, which opened in 1895.

In the 1890s, when the glen had its heyday as a fun park, entertainments provided by entrepreneur Sam Wilson included a big dipper called the Ocean Switchback, reminiscent of days at Scarborough, and a toboggan slide which took passengers up and down the sides of the glen. The slide was closed after a crash in 1900.

Bingley can be approached by canal, railway and road from Saltaire, and is about two miles to the north-west of Salt's village. It is now a commuter town for Bradford, but nonetheless boasts a few interesting idiosyncrasies. It was home to Titus Salt junior, son of Sir Titus. The site of his mansion was Milner Field, halfway between Saltaire and Bingley, almost immediately north of the Aire where it passes under the canal.

For his architect young Titus chose Thomas Harris rather than his father's favourites Lockwood and Mawson, and Harris built the monumental towered Gothic pile Milner Field for his client in 1871-3. Harris used cavity wall construction and raised the whole edifice on a terrace. Salt designed the conservatories himself, and spared no expense on the interior decoration. There was furniture in the Gothic style by Charles Bevan, glass by Saunders & Co, and carvings by Thomas Nicholls. Sadly this fantastic abode was in decay by the 1950s and has now been demolished.

There are locks on the canal just west of Milner Field, more locks in the centre of Bingley, beside the Italianate mill to the north of the station, and Five Rise Locks at Crossflatts half a mile further north. Access to Five Rise Locks is from Canal Road, Crossflatts (about half a mile from Crossflatts Station), or by the well-walked towpath which takes the traveller from the mills of Bingley to the heart of the country in a trice. These five staircase locks (there is no neutral water between them) raise the canal up almost eighty-eight feet eight inches, a major engineering feat. The Bingley to Skipton section of the Leeds & Liverpool Canal was opened on the 13th April 1773.

A surprising and surviving mansion stands only half a mile from Five Rise Locks as the crow flies, but earth-bound explorers must take Beck Lane at the Canal Road roundabout, go left at the main Park Road and second left into Lady Lane.

Here is Oakwood, a piece of unexciting Victorian Tudor on the outside but hiding interior work by William Burges. The house was built for Thomas Garnett by Bradford architects George Knowles and William Wilcox in 1864, with William Morris and Edward Burne-Jones contributing stained glass designs on a Chaucerian theme for the staircase window the following year. Burges was commissioned to design furnishings for two rooms. Of this, the dining room fireplace has survived, a massive, castellated carved-stone overmantel by Thomas Nicholls bearing the initials TG and an imp-like figure.

Head west from Bingley on the B6429, which leads towards Harden and Cullingworth, and passes through the pretty valley of Harden Beck. It is overlooked by a folly which has made its way into literature, as the model for the folly 'very solidly built' by Peregrine St Clair in Bradford-born John Braine's *Room at the Top*, published in 1957. The real folly, St Davids Ruin, is a mile out of Bingley and about half a mile south of the Harden road near the Malt Shovel pub. It can be reached by following Beck Foot Lane, half a mile west of Bingley on the B6429, south then taking the footpath which leads southwest at Beck Foot Mill. The path leads up the hill into Ruin Bank Wood.

St Davids Ruin was built on its hilly site in 1796 by Benjamin Ferrand to act as an eyecatcher for his house St Ives, designed by James Paine in 1759, which stood across the valley to the north. St Ives has been demolished but the ruin of St Davids has endured, the artfully crumbling tower and arch a fine model for folly builders.

The Black Hills at Harden mark the edge of Bradford Dale. Many footpaths cross the lesser-known moors and hills between Harden and Calderdale to the south-west, and the

Black Dyke Mills at Queensbury are a monumental reminder of the power of coal and textiles in the south of the dale. Queensbury is eight miles from Harden along the B6429, A629 and A644; the small, stone-built village is completely dominated by John Foster & Sons' mill, built in 1835.

A mile east, heading back to Bradford on the A647 at Clayton Heights, is the huge, rusticated-stone arched entrance to Highgate Mills (1851 and 1862). The arch, with a giant head as keystone, and accompanying terraces of workers' cottages date from 1865. The mill and housing formed a small self-contained community; even decorative cast iron posts for mounting washing lines were provided. Was this an early form of advertising? Doubtless many of the clothes hanging on the lines would once have been made in Bradford, but much has changed in the textile trade and the dale itself since Worstedopolis was at the height of its powers.

A SKYLINE OF TOWERS

Along the Calder Valley

S tanding atop the grassy earthworks of Sandal Castle, a mile south of Wakefield (off the A61), the traveller takes in the fine view of the towers, spires and domes of the hillside town across the Calder in the knowledge that the Battle of Wakefield was fought close to the castle over 500 years ago. The earthworks date from the eleventh or twelfth century but the keep, of which a little masonry remains above ground, was built after 1328.

Its crucial role in the War of the Roses came about after the defeat of Henry VI at Northampton in July 1460; the king was taken prisoner by the Yorkists and the Duke of York made heir to the crown by the Act of Settlement.

This state of affairs displeased the king's mother, Queen Margaret, who rallied Lancastrian troops in the north, while the Yorkists responded by marching from London to Sandal Castle in mid-December 1460. Feeding this army of between 5,000 and 12,000 men was beyond the resources of the castle,

and so foraging parties went out to raid the local countryside.

For their part, the Lancastrians did not have the capacity to besiege the castle in winter, and resorted to trickery. A truce was declared until Epiphany and promptly broken on the 30th December when the Yorkists were lured from the castle and overwhelmed by the enemy. The duke and over 2,000 of his men were killed, thus securing, at least for a time, the succession for young Edward, Prince of Wales.

At the time of the battle, Wakefield was an important weaving and dyeing centre. It first rose to prosperity in the thirteenth century but never became as industrialised as many other West Riding towns; it had collieries, but its market, dating from 1204, gained in importance as the clothing trade declined, and Leeds and Bradford overtook Wakefield as textile centres. Wakefield, county town of the West Riding, thus has a different emphasis about its buildings: fewer warehouses and factories, more Georgian houses and later

Sandal Castle, with Wakefield in the distance.

administrative buildings, and in general a more expansive feel which partly results from its hilly site.

Below the city to the south and east runs the Calder, its great loop to the north-east removed in 1839 when the Aire & Calder Navigation's new cut between Castleford and Wakefield was opened, removing five miles off the river distance between the two. At Stanley Ferry, cut crosses river by aqueduct, probably the largest cast iron aqueduct in the world. It is 165 feet in length and holds 940 tons of water. The road linking the A642 from Wakefield with Altofts crosses both cut and river just to the north of the aqueduct.

Westgate, in the centre of Wakefield, was a fashionable residential area in the late eighteenth century. The four Milnes brothers,

Wakefield cloth merchants, brick makers and timber importers, hired John Carr to build town houses on Westgate, but all their splendid mansions were destroyed when the original station was built in 1867.

The clear destination on Westgate is the cathedral, but pause a moment to admire the glorious ceramic façade of a pub, the Elephant and Castle, before passing by the Opera House, the smallest of Frank Matcham's surviving theatres. It was built in 1894 on the site of the Theatre Royal (1775-6), which stood amongst the merchants' houses and was well patronised by county families (although the backstage facilities were awful). Matcham's Opera House cost £13,000 and seated around 700 people; he decorated the gabled façade with busts of authors and composers, and the domed auditorium with masses of Rococo plasterwork. Only forty-five feet separate front of stage from rear of stalls in this intimate theatre.

At the east end of Westgate stands the cathedral, until 1888 simply the parish church of All Saints. The combined tower and spire reach 247 feet in height, the tallest in Yorkshire. The site was home to Saxon then Norman churches, but when the crossing tower of the Norman church collapsed around 1315, extensive rebuilding took place. It was complete in 1329, although the church had no tower; around seventy years later, parishoners were asked to contribute to a fund for a bell tower. Money began to flow in only after the Archbishop of York offered four days' indulgence, or remission from the punishments of purgatory, in exchange for financial assistance. By 1420 a tower of 105 feet topped by a crocketed spire of 142 feet was under construction. The decorative crocketing in

leaf shapes gives the handsome spire a serrated appearance.

Further rebuilding and additions followed over the centuries, but by 1857 the fabric had become so worn that Sir George Gilbert Scott was called in to advise on restoration, which took place during 1858-74. This resulted in the loss of old furnishings and details such as mason-marks on stonework, but the fine carved screen of 1635 was allowed to remain. As befitting its cathedral status, a new chancel and transept were commisioned from John Loughborough Pearson after 1888, but his death in 1897 meant that the work was undertaken by his son. Frederick Loughborough Pearson produced a design in his father's manner, emphasising the vertical elements leading to an elaborate vault, which was built in 1904.

Another Wakefield tower of note crowns the town hall to the north-west of the cathedral in Wood Street. The town hall was built in 1877-80 in Tudor style with large oriel bay windows, but it is the 190 foot campanile which dominates the design by London architect Thomas Collcutt. Collcutt bettered the height of his Wakefield tower in 1887-93 when he produced the 280 foot tower of the Imperial Institute in South Kensington, though this was far from Italianate.

Also on Wood Street is a competing tower, though only 130 feet high, its domed cupola marking the entrance to the West Riding County Hall(1893-8). The style is an eclectic version of Queen Anne Revival by architects Gibson and Russell, who also built the Middlesex County Offices. Lucky visitors to the domed council chamber will be rewarded with a glimpse of a perfect turn of the century

The West Riding County Hall on Wood Street, Wakefield, with the court house in the foreground.

municipal interior, complete with original Art Nouveau light fittings.

Down below the civic centre of Wakefield, on the medieval Old Bridge over the Calder, stands Wakefield's most unusual building, the chantry chapel of St Mary-on-the-Bridge. It occupies a tiny island in the Calder, its west front aligned with the bridge parapet. It was built in the 1340s when bridge chapels - partly shrines, partly a means of collecting money for upkeep of the bridge - were not uncommon. Now, however, it is the best of the four such chapels remaining in England, with Decorated tracery on its north, east and south façades, and five elaborate arches facing the bridge. The chapel became sorely neglected by the seventeenth century and was later used, amongst other purposes, for selling old clothes; its restoration in 1847 was something of a comedy, starring Sir George Gilbert Scott and a local mason.

Scott intended to repair the badly-damaged west front, but the mason persuaded him to allow the entire west façade to be transported four miles south to Kettlethorpe Hall and replaced by a replica carved by the aforesaid mason. The replica decayed rapidly and itself had to be restored in 1932. The original façade became part of a boathouse on the serpentine lake at Kettlethorpe (now part of New-millerdam Country Park on the A61 south of Sandal Castle), a romantic situation in which it decayed rather more slowly than the imposter. After this farce, it is a surprise that Scott was let loose on the parish church.

Only one mile east of the Old Bridge is the remarkable village of Heath, where mansions edge the rough hilltop common, a Yorkshire forerunner of Regents Park. There are two large houses, Heath House and Heath Hall, but in addition this model village for the monied classes of the eighteenth century has assorted cottages, stables, the Dower House (one reserved for a widow) and a seventeenth century water tower. Until its demolition in 1960 the Old Hall, a small Elizabethan prodigy

Wakefield Town Hall.

house based on a Robert Smythson design, stood close by. Now all that remains of this excellent but neglected house are the gates, with pineapple finials topping the piers. The wealthy were probably attracted to Heath Common as it combined proximity to Wakefield with a spacious site and good views; it was satisfactory in both aspect and prospect.

Heath House was built in 1744 by a young James Paine, who rebuilt an existing house as an exercise in Palladianism on a small scale. Heath Hall is much the biggest structure on the common, and it, too, is a result of rebuilding. The architect was John Carr, who was employed from around 1754 to enlarge Eshald House (later renamed Heath Hall) which had been designed and built in 1694-1703 by its owner, Theophilus Shelton, Registrar of Deeds in the West Riding. Carr remodelled the original house, and added wings and detached pavilions at either side, the works extending until 1780 and producing a memorable ensemble of buildings. The interior decoration was also of a high standard, with the drawing room stretching along the entire north wing.

John Carr was born in 1723 at Horbury, three miles south-west of Wakefield. At least three previous generations of Carrs had owned quarries and worked as stonemasons at Horbury, and John followed the family tradition. He began to design houses during the late 1740s, and, although he never had any formal architectural training, built up his country house practice until by the late eighteenth century he was the leading architect in Yorkshire and the north of England. He died in 1807 and was buried at the church of St Peter and St Leonard at Horbury, which was rebuilt in 1791-3 at Carr's expense and to his own design. The church is a cool, Classical design with a portico of four attached Ionic columns, but the dominant feature is the tower which rises layer upon layer to be topped by a conical spire. The temple-like interior has apses at either end. It was an important and influential church in terms of ecclesiastical design.

Two miles upstream from Horbury along the Calder lies Thornhill and its ruined fifteenth century manor house Thornhill Hall, once the home of the Savile family.

The B6117 runs between the church of St Michael and the manor house, but Thornhill may also be approached along the canal towpath from Horbury via Horbury Bridge over the Calder. The canal is part of the Calder & Hebble Navigation which made the Calder navigable between Wakefield and Sowerby Bridge; it was begun in 1759 and fully opened in 1770.

Though Thornhill Hall retains its moat, it cannot compete in extravagance as a monument to the Saviles with the church, which hides a magnificent array of family memorials. Its Savile Chapel was built by Sir Thomas Savile in 1447 and enlarged in 1493. Inside, figures of Sir John (died 1481) and his wife lie on a tomb chest, Sir George (died 1622) is sheltered by a canopy, effigies of Sir George (died 1614) and his wife are prone under a huge monument, and an oak tomb contains Sir John (died 1504) and his two wives. This is a splendid set of finely-crafted memorials, and in addition to these sculptural riches, the chapel retains much fifteenth century glass; the chancel east window also has a restored Tree of Jesse dating from 1499, showing Christ's genealogy.

A four mile journey west from Thornhill takes the traveller from Savile to Beaumont territory and the site of the Beaumont family home, Whitley Beaumont in Whitley Park, west of the B6118 between Kirkheaton and Grange Moor.

Several Beaumont monuments may be found in the Beaumont Chapel of the church of St John at Kirkheaton, while in the churchyard a column stands as a memorial to seventeen children who died in a mill fire at Colne Bridge, a mile or so to the north, in 1818.

The Whitley Beaumont mansion was demolished in 1952, but occupying the highest point of Whitley Park is a now roofless garden temple, probably designed by James Paine in 1752-4 while he was working on the house for his brother-in-law Richard Beaumont.

The A644, across the Calder from Kirkheaton, leads quickly into Dewsbury and thence Batley. These are textile towns, once packed with mills and rows of terraces. The best building in Dewsbury is undoubtedly the town hall, designed by local architects Henry Holtom and George Fox in 1888-89 on what could be called the Leeds principle, that is with a dominating tower. On the western edge of the town centre is the heavily Tudor railway station, built in 1848 (and extended in 1889); nearby are some good mid-nineteenth century Italianate warehouses.

In Batley the Bagshaw Museum at Wilton Park (off the A652 heading north-west) is housed in Victorian millowner George Sheard's eccentric Gothic mansion, replete with many original decorative details. The Woodlands, as it was originally known, was built in 1875 to the design of Sheard and local architect Walter Hanstock, and cost £25,000. Interiors on the ground floor still retain their fine wood-carving and painting; the dining room frieze shows a medieval feast in progress. After Sheard died in 1902 the house was eventually sold for only £5 and became a museum in 1911, local JP Walter Bagshaw being the driving force behind the scheme.

A little further out along the A652 is Oakwell Hall, a moated manor house dating from 1583 (with later alterations), which is now the focus of a country park. The house has a large central hall, typical of the group of Pennine manor houses built in the early to mid-seventeenth century, which were financed from the profits of farming and the cloth trade.

The architectural masterpiece of nearby Heckmondwike, on the western edge of Batley, stems neither from mills nor the municipality but Nonconformism.

Heckmondwike's Upper Independent Chapel was built for the town Congregationalists in 1898-9 and designed by Arthur Stott, a Heckmondwike man who was more than likely a Nonconformist himself. It is a vast cathedral of dissent in an inflated Classical style, with a giant Corinthian portico and Baroque ornamentation; sadly, very little of the galleried interior with its fine plasterwork now remains.

These gigantic Nonconformist halls of worship often completely outshone local parish churches in size and ornamentation, and perhaps an element of inter-town competition entered into late Victorian chapel-building, as certainly occurred in the case of town halls. At one time demolition seemed to

The arms of the Lancashire & Yorkshire Railway Company on the southern pavilion of Huddersfield Station.

be the fate of the Upper Independent Chapel, but a change of use now appears more likely.

Take the A62 south from Heckmondwike to Huddersfield, or better still catch the southbound train from Batley or Dewsbury, and emerge at Huddersfield in front of the grandest Classical station façade in the country. The centrepiece of the 416 foot frontage is a giant six-column Corinthian portico; the pavilions at either end carry different coats of arms, those of the Lancashire & Yorkshire Railway and the Huddersfield &

Manchester Railway & Canal Company. These two companies, joint promoters of the station which was built in 1846-50, each occupied a pavilion but shared the platforms and all the usual station facilities. Today the station itself only occupies a tiny portion of this magnificent structure.

The architect was James Pigott Pritchett the elder of York, a man best-known for his ecclesiastical work and at first sight not an obvious choice of designer for a railway station; in fact Huddersfield was Pritchett's sole station. But Pritchett, a prominent Congregationalist, had carried out occasional commissions in Huddersfield since 1824 and was widely-known throughout Yorkshire. Perhaps this combination persuaded the railway companies that he could produce a fitting façade for their station, which stands at the centre of a magnificent collection of tunnels and viaducts, occasioned by Huddersfield's position at the junction of three valleys. Best are the twenty-arch Longwood Viaduct (1849) on the Manchester line along the Colne Valley, and the Lockwood Viaduct (1849) which carries the Sheffield line 122 feet above the River Holme just south of Lockwood Station.

Huddersfield has its roots in the domestic weaving trade. A market was established in the town in 1672 and a cloth hall built in 1766 by the lord of the manor, Sir John Ramsden. Industrial expansion in the eighteenth and nineteenth centuries concentrated on fine worsted production. The Ramsdens were highly influential in the development of Huddersfield. They owned the Ramsden Estate, which accounted for much of the town centre and was eventually bought by the corporation in 1920; thus Huddersfield became 'the town that bought itself'.

The Ramsdens were also involved in bringing canal and railway links to the town. Sir John Ramsden's Canal, a broad one with nine locks linking the town to the Calder & Hebble Navigation, was built in 1774-6. The Ramsdens had every incentive to assist the town's growth, as in 1774 they owned all but one of the houses in the town, and a third of the land through which the canal was to be driven. The Huddersfield Canal, which took only narrow boats, later connected the town

The bridge and mill at Quay Street, reflected in Sir John Ramsden's Canal.

with Manchester via the Ashton Canal. Ramsden's Canal is still navigable and the Huddersfield Canal is currently undergoing restoration; its towpath may be walked from near the town centre to Tunnel End near Marsden, where the canal disappears beneath a narrow neck of the Pennines.

Huddersfield's architectural attractions are spread widely in terms of geography and taste, ranging from the warehouses, locks and bridges of the canal to a pair of turn of the century towers. The pick of the buildings in the original centre of Huddersfield, which lay to the south of the railway station, is the wonderfully uplifting Brook Street Market, a piece of Victorian hi-tech in cast iron with glazed curtain walls. It was built in 1887-8 by the town's borough surveyor Richard Swarbrick Dugdale to house the wholesale market, and has survived restoration to serve as a popular general market. Its light, airy and

Brook Street Market in Huddersfield.

translucent presence raises the spirits and enhances the press of activities beneath the canopy.

The town hall on Princess Street is a Baroque pile designed by Dugdale's predecessor as borough surveyor, John Abbey, and built in 1878-81. Byram Arcade, close to the station on Westgate, was built by the Ramsden Estate Company in 1880-1; two to three levels of balconies rise above the ground floor shops in a vertiginous piece of design by W H Crossland. The elegant, faintly Art Deco façade of the Wellington public house greets the shopper emerging from the arcade on to Westgate.

The area north of the old town centre was developed from 1845, as cloth traders abandoned the market atmosphere of the cloth hall for individual custom-built warehouses which were erected on the Ramsden Estate near the new St Georges Square in front of the railway station. They were stone-built and Italianate in style, with offices on the street front and the warehouse functions to the rear; some survive on John William Street, just east of the station.

Not all developments in this area were Classical merchant's palaces, however: the railway's Goods & Wool Warehouse (1878-83), overlooking the rear of the station, was built for the textile trade in solid red-brick. The structural oddity beside it, a brick box raised on giant columns, is a wagon hoist used to lift entire railway wagons to the second floor of the building, where they were moved on a tram-like system to loading bays.

North-west of the station, residential developments spread up New North Road, uphill into Edgerton and Lindley, where villas and mansions hid in a woodland setting far above industrial Huddersfield; there is a 1,000 foot drop in height between the western and eastern edges of the town.

W H Armitage's house Banney Royd, off Halifax Road, was designed in 1890 by Edgar Wood of Manchester in a combination of

The interior of Brook Street Market.

The splendid Victorian façade of the Elephant and Castle in Wakefield.

Tudor and Art Nouveau styles, which happily married traditional Yorkshire taste with Wood's quirky modernity. Wood, the Nonconformist son of a cotton millowner, acquired a reputation for stylistic innovation, exemplified by his Clock Tower in the centre of nearby Lindley (up Daisy Lea Road from Halifax Road). This jolly 1902 work was commissioned by local millowner James Nield Sykes.

Four miles to the south-east, across the Colne and Holme valleys, stands another tower, the Victoria Tower on Castle Hill. The 900 foot high Castle Hill was inhabited 4,000 years ago and is the site of an Iron Age fort built by the Brigantes, the tribe of northern

The wagon hoist at Huddersfield's Goods and Wool Warehouse, beside the railway station.

The Wainhouse Tower.

England. A series of huge ramparts ring the hilltop, which was occupied until the Roman conquest of the Brigantes, whereupon it was deserted for 1,000 years. A castle was built on the site in the 1140s by the de Laci family, but this was taken down by Henry III, and the hill was finally crowned by the Victoria Tower, marking the queen's jubilee, in 1897-8. It cost £3,398 to build and was just over 100 feet high.

The turreted tower was designed by William Wallen of Huddersfield, a Ramsden estate architect, and those who manage to climb its 165 steps will enjoy a tremendous view of the surrounding countryside. (The tower is open on summer afternoons.) To the north-east may be seen the pretty village of Almondbury, a weaving village which boasted a market in the thirteenth century, well before Huddersfield. Its All Hallows Church has a fine ceiling with decorated bosses, some showing grotesque faces, which was built in 1522 by one Geferay Daystre. The canopied font cover is a fine example of fifteenth century workmanship.

Looking north-west from the Victoria Tower on Castle Hill, the expansive view beyond Huddersfield takes in the most memorable tower in Calderdale, the Wainhouse Tower on the southern edge of Halifax. This monument to personal aggrandisement and the fortunes of industry can be seen for miles around. It stands, like a triffid in a back garden, on the southern edge of Halifax almost beside the busy A646 Skircoat Moor Road where it meets the A58 route to the town centre; a path leads south-west from the junction down through trees to the tower.

The 253 foot high Wainhouse Tower was originally intended as a chimney for the

Washer Lane dyeworks of local industrialist John Edward Wainhouse (1817-83). Halifax architect Isaac Booth drew up plans for the chimney, which was to be connected to the works by a pipeline, and building work began on the octagonal structure in 1871. As both chimney and costs rose ever higher, Wainhouse sold his dyeworks but kept the chimney, which he decided to turn into an observatory.

Meanwhile, his architect had been persuaded to stop work by Sir Harry Edwards, who owned the adjoining estate and was currently pursuing a feud with Wainhouse. Wainhouse immediately engaged Booth's former pupil Richard Dugdale (later to be found in Huddersfield) to complete the tower, and this he did in some style with a decorative Renaissance pavilion, finished in 1875. The total cost was in the region of £15,000. The public are invited to climb the tower's 403 steps, which spiral upward around the inner chimney casing, on only about eight days in each year.

The Halifax of 1875 had come far from its origins as a small community on the banks of Hebble Brook, a tributary of the Calder. In the fourteenth century it was only a small village, but by the second half of the fifteenth century the town had become an important textile centre. A cloth hall existed in the sixteenth century, and Halifax was in the same league as Leeds and well ahead of Bradford in terms of the cloth trade by the mid-seventeenth century.

Turnpike roads began to connect Halifax with its neighbours from 1734 onwards, and the Halifax branch of the Calder & Hebble Navigation opened in 1828. The branch, running parallel with Hebble Brook for a mile and three-quarters from Salterhebble to the Halifax basin, was a difficult and costly undertaking, with fourteen locks in a rise of just over 100 feet. Almost £59,000 was spent on the work by the Navigation company, which hoped to profit from increased tolls from local traders, who might use the branch rather than carrying their goods to Sowerby Bridge.

The population of Halifax grew from 20,000 in 1841 to 82,000 in 1891, making the town of today essentially Victorian in character. Its plan is largely a grid pattern of terraces interspersed with mills and other works, but although an industrial town it has a spectacular setting and a few surprises in store for the traveller, particularly the wealth of Classical architecture.

The small, modern railway station, beside the original 1855 Classical station designed for the Lancashire & Yorkshire Railway, makes a useful starting point as it brings the visitor immediately to Church Street. To the right and a few yards north is Square Road and the soaring spire of Square Congregational Church. Tower and spire together reach about 235 feet in height, dominating the surrounding buildings.

The church was designed by Joseph James of London in 1857 to replace the neighbouring Square Chapel(1771-2). When built, Square Chapel was the largest and most splendid place of Nonconformist worship in the country. Its ruddy-pink brick façade is still imposing, and the once-abandoned building underwent conversion to an arts centre in 1992.

The newer Gothic church was as splendid a building as the chapel. James decorated the

Square Chapel, Halifax, seen through the rose window in the ruins of Square Congregational Church.

transepts with rose windows and used the east window of Selby Abbey as a model for part of his west façade. The body of the church cost £15,000, but the tower and spire were given by Sir Frank Crossley of the Halifax family of carpet magnates. Sadly the church suffered severe fire damage in 1970 and was later largely demolished, but the gloriously exaggerated spire still towers over the town.

Behind Square Church are the forbidding blank stone walls of the superlative Piece Hall, eighteenth century architecture at its best. Entry to the cloth hall, through a grand archway, is from the south or west, so retreat

Halifax Piece Hall.

The gates of the Piece Hall.

The Borough Market, Halifax.

back along Square Road, turn right into Blackledge and right again; before you stands a monumental quadrangle, a vast open space (over 90,000 square feet) enclosed by two to three storeys of galleried arcades on a sloping site. It was erected in 1774-9 and John Hope of Liverpool was the architect. All is elegant stonework, and the gallery pillars diminish in width from floor to floor, the top tier being Tuscan columns. The ground floor was known as the Rustic, the middle floor as the Arcade and the top as the Colonnade. The cloth merchants were housed in 315 separate rooms, each with its own door and window.

The Piece Hall became a wholesale fruit, vegetable and fish market in 1871, after the trading requirements of the cloth merchants changed, and recent restoration has enabled the building to continue in use with shops, retail markets and entertainments. Thus the Piece Hall now is something of a stage set, but nothing can detract from the quality of its architecture.

West of the Piece Hall across Market Street stands the Borough Market, built in 1891-8 by local architects John and Joseph Leeming. The stone-built exterior, a Renaissance accumulation of shops and flats, hides an airy and highly-decorative cast iron and glass interior, with a central octagon over sixty feet in height. Four avenues of stalls radiate from the octagon, which is marked by an elegant clock-cum-lamp standard rising above the stalls. This retail market was built by the corporation on the site of an old open market, the intention being to complement the wholesale market activities at the Piece Hall after its change of use.

Looking north up Market Street, the tower of the town hall - a tall and wonderfully over-decorated French Gothic confection - is unmistakable. It was built in 1859-63, but the matter of a town hall had been discussed locally from around 1847.

John Crossley of the carpet family was mayor of Halifax in 1850-1, and then, at his own expense, began to clear an area of the old town around Northgate on which he erected several palatial Italianate commercial buildings. He left a suitable site for the new town hall, which he suggested should be in the same style. This provoked controversy and competing designs, including one from local textile manufacturer Edward Akroyd using the Gothic style. Some years of argument

Halifax Town Hall.

ensued, mingling personal pride with debate on the correct built form for municipal offices in a democratic society, until in 1859 Sir Charles Barry was asked to design the building.

Barry, who was still working on the Houses of Parliament, first defined his ideal town hall then produced a plan for a monumental towered building, externally imposing and internally colourful with lavish marble, stone and tilework. He died in 1860, without seeing either the Houses of Parliament or Halifax Town Hall completed, and his son Edward

Middleton Barry finished off the Halifax work by adding the mansard roof. The Prince of Wales opened the town hall in 1863, perhaps bringing about a brief truce in the battle for architectural prestige being fought between local textile manufacturers, the fruits of which may be visited in the outskirts of Halifax.

But first, a modern monument to money: just to the west of the town hall and Borough Market is Commercial Street, where the monstrous lozenge of the Halifax Building Society's new offices bursts upon the Victorian

Decorative ironwork inside the Borough Market, Halifax.

Head office building under construction for the Halifax Building Society in June 1972.

The Halifax Building Society offices.

townscape. The structure, a vast diamond-shaped block raised well above street level on massive concrete legs, was built in 1972-5 by the Building Design Partnership. It has brutal magnificence and confidence, but lacks the decorative splendour that eventually endeared the great nineteenth century piles to the public. Despite this it is certainly memorable, even unforgettable.

To see the built outcome of the wars of the textile magnates, follow Northgate past the town hall and further north along North Bridge. Take the subway left under the ring road to Haley Hill; less than a quarter of a mile up the hill on the right is All Souls Church, and before it the statue of its benefactor Colonel Edward Akroyd, holding a plan of the village he sees before him and inviting the passer-by to admire it - Akroydon.

The first Akroyd venture into workers' housing was not Akroydon but Copley, on the southern edge of Halifax close to the river and navigation (access is from the A6026 Wakefield Road, near the splendid Copley railway viaduct). James Akroyd & Son, the country's leading worsted spinners, bought Copley Mill in 1844 and began Copley model village in 1847 to provide their workers with decent housing near to their place of work. By 1865 the village of stone-built terraces was completed, with a school, shops, library and church, at no small cost to the firm.

The largest Akroyd mill was on Haley Hill, and in 1859 Edward Akroyd commissioned George Gilbert Scott to produce a village plan for the area, to be known as Akroydon; the Gothic style was selected to blend in with the Halifax vernacular. Assorted terraces and pairs of houses were soon built near All Souls,

The new Halifax Building Society head offices loom over Commercial Street in the 1970s.

a Scott design erected in 1856-9. The church is a fine example of High Victorian, with a tower reaching 236 feet in height. The interior was full of colour, combining painted decoration, polished granite, marble, mosaic and stained glass, all to designs by top craftsmen. The chancel and monumental pulpit are quite extravagant.

The Crossley model village was built in the same era, at West Hill Park overlooking the Crossley mills a quarter mile to the north-east down in the valley of Hebble Brook. The octagonal 321 foot chimney of Crossley's Dean Clough Mill (1857) is still a landmark.

West Hill Park is west of the town centre, around Gibbet Street and Hopwood Lane; from the town hall, take Broad Street to the west and cross the ring road via Pellon Lane. A left into New Brunswick Street will bring you out on to Gibbet Street. The horrific gibbet, a form of guillotine used until 1650 to behead those who stole cloth worth over 13d, still stands on the street. It claimed fifty victims. The Crossleys initially laid out the People's Park, just to the south, in 1856-7 and John Crossley began building West Hill Park village near the park in 1863. Stone terraces in Tudor and Gothic styles reach north to Gibbet Street.

The motives behind these and similar model village schemes like Titus Salt's Saltaire were a mixture of straightforward philanthropy, acute business sense, civic pride and responsibility (often inspired by religious belief), and a certain amount of interpersonal competition, the latter a particularly important element in Halifax. For the millworkers the outcome was generally an improvement in living conditions without too many onerous estate regulations, and future generations

were bequeathed a variety of architecturally interesting villages in the midst of Northern industrial towns. The need for model villages was disappearing even as they were built, for the mid-nineteenth century saw the start of the building society movement, which aimed to enable working people to buy their own homes.

Sowerby Bridge lies only a couple of miles upstream from Copley along the Calder, at the point where the River Ryburn enters from the south. The little town developed in the eighteenth and nineteenth centuries, as its easy access to canal and rail transport brought it prosperity in contrast to the original hilltop village of Sowerby, a mile to the west, which went into decline.

The canal wharf and warehouses at Sowerby Bridge are attractive, but Sowerby boasts the grandiose church of St Peter, one of the best Classical churches in the north of England. It was built in 1763-6 to replace its small and decaying predecessor; congregations had been decreasing as potential worshippers attended chapel instead of the old church. The massive Corinthian columns of its interior resemble those of Holy Trinity, Leeds, on which Halifax master-mason John Wilson based his design for St Peter. The wonderfully ornate display of plasterwork in the apse is by Giuseppe Cortese, who worked on several of the great Yorkshire country houses.

Hebden Bridge, like Sowerby Bridge, benefited from its position in the Calder Valley as first the Rochdale Canal (1804) and then the railway (1841) used this relatively low-level route across the Pennines. The town's first stone bridge was built around 1510, replacing

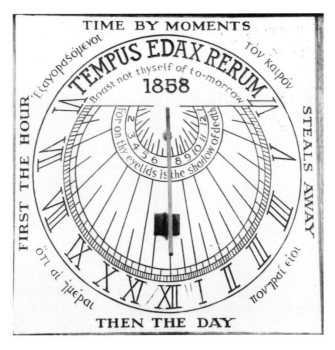

A sundial in the People's Park, Halifax.

a wooden bridge dating from the fourteenth century, but Hebden Bridge really began to develop with the building of steam-powered mills in the nineteenth century. Sandstone terraces of worker's cottages line the steep hills of the little town, with some tall terraces having entrances for each floor at different levels on the hillside.

Hebden Bridge sits astride Hebden Water; to the west, looking down on valley and town, is the hilltop village of Heptonstall, predecessor of Hebden Bridge as a textile centre. Several paths and lanes take the walker or driver the steep half mile up Cross Hill between the two settlements.

A pair of churches stand just to the southwest of the main crossroads in Heptonstall, the old and new Churches of St Thomas. The old church dates back to the thirteenth century, but following its partial collapse caused by storm damage in 1847, the church was dismantled in 1854. The ruins stand across the churchyard from the new church, which was built in 1849-54. In the graveyard of the new church lies the writer Sylvia Plath, who died in 1963. The American-born Plath married poet Ted Hughes, who had spent his youth in the Calder Valley, in 1956.

The alternative place of worship in Heptonstall was the Wesleyan chapel, situated to the north of the churches in Northgate. Early Wesleyan meetings were held in the open air, but when Methodist preachers were prevented from using churches, the construction of meeting houses became essential. They were generally small, rectangular buildings, but the Heptonstall chapel is octagonal, a form which allowed the preacher to be in the centre of the congregation. It was built in 1764 using roof timbers made by a carpenter who had previously worked on a similar chapel in Rotherham. The roof sections were brought by packhorse from Rotherham using the high moorland route. The chapel was partially rebuilt in 1802 but the octagonal form and internal gallery were retained.

The handsome stone-built houses of Heptonstall and other villages in the upper Calder Valley are largely a product of the rebuilding which began in the late sixteenth century and extended into the seventeenth and eighteenth centuries.

The upper Calder Valley is particularly rich in sizeable houses of this era because of the wealth of yeomen-clothiers who combined farming with work in the textile industry; farmers holding land in the lower part of the valley, to the east of Halifax, were more reliant on agriculture, and were generally poorer. Entry into the textile trade was easy, with the cost of a loom at the end of the seventeenth century as little as £1, and return on capital outlay was rapid.

One such yeoman-clothier was Robert Sutcliffe, who died in 1718 leaving goods worth £679 and a fine house at Greenwood Lee, a mile and a half north-west of Heptonstall on the lane overlooking Hebden Dale, the valley of Hebden Water (keep right at Slack). The house bears the date 1712, although it may be of earlier construction, and has a superb array of mullioned windows and ball finials, with a decorative stepped window on the gable end which originally held the doorway. Sutcliffe was both a farmer and a merchant; he left a stock of eighty-six undyed kerseys (a coarse woollen cloth) valued at £151.

Just past Greenwood Lee to the north are a car park and picnic spot where a path leads down into Hebden Dale, reaching Hebden Water opposite a nineteenth century cotton mill. Barely half a mile up the valley, via various woodland walks, lie the attractive outcrops of Hardcastle Crags.

Back in the narrow Calder Valley, road, railway and canal are squeezed tightly together between Hebden Bridge and Todmorden, the next settlement of note upstream. Travellers through the valley will see another of Calderdale's towers on the skyline to the south, the obelisk of Stoodley Pike, which stands on the moors two miles to the east of Todmorden.

The original monument was built by public subscription to commemorate the surrender of Paris during the Napoleonic Wars in 1814, but it collapsed in 1854. The worthies of Todmorden decided that it should be replaced, and asked local architect James Green for a design; his 120 foot high obelisk cost £812 and was completed in 1856. This coincided with the end of the Crimean War, for which the pike then served as a peace memorial. Stoodley Pike is visible for miles around and stands on the route of the Pennine Way; those wishing to see Calderdale from the pike could use the footpath leading up from London Road, which leaves Mankinholes to the north-east.

Mankinholes and the nearby village of Lumbutts may both be reached by lanes leading south from the A646 valley road as it touches the eastern edge of Todmorden. In Lumbutts is a unique tower, the wheelhouse of Lumbutts Mill, which once contained three overshot water wheels, one above the other. The water was supplied from the series of small reservoirs to the south and dropped from wheel to wheel, generating a maximum of over fifty horsepower. The wheelhouse was probably built around 1830 to power a cotton spinning mill.

Todmorden evolved at the junction of the Calder Valley and a smaller valley to the south, which was eventually used by both canal and railway as a trans-Pennine route. The buildings of Todmorden, another product of the industrial revolution in Calderdale, are strung out along the sides of this T-shaped depression. The Rochdale Canal was opened in 1804 and the railway to Manchester in 1841, providing Todmorden industrialists with links to wider markets. Foremost amongst the country's cotton manufacturers in the early nineteenth century was John Fielden (1784-1849) of Todmorden, Unitarian and philanthropist, whose finance and influence lay behind the construction of the town's three monumental buildings.

The Unitarian church, immediately south of Fielden Square, was given by the sons of John Fielden and built in 1865-9. With its tall spire and rich interior, resplendent with polished granite arcades, the church is far more imposing than the parish church. The architect was John Gibson, who briefly worked for Sir Charles Barry but is best known as the designer of several buildings for the National Provincial Bank.

The Fieldens ensured that the commission for Todmorden Town Hall (1870-5) - a little to the north of Fielden Square - also went to Gibson, and he responded with a Classical temple on a small scale, though its giant Corinthian columns appear large in this setting. The sculptured figures in the pediment symbolise the industries of Yorkshire and Lancashire.

The Fielden family mansion Dobroyd Castle hovers above the town on the hillside to the west. It was built for John Fielden junior in 1866-9, again by John Gibson, who designed a castellated villa which is most impressive at a distance. The staircase, though, has columns galore, stained glass and carvings depicting cotton manufacturing and the life of John Fielden senior.

The valley to the south of Todmorden is notable for two heroic feats of engineering, the Rochdale Canal (1804) and the Manchester & Leeds Railway (1841). Although the railway's engineer was George Stephenson, his assistant, Thomas L Gooch, was actually responsible for most of the line. Gooch, a reliable engineer who never had complete charge of building a main line, retired in 1851 when only forty-two because of illness caused by overwork.

The canal towpath is accessible from the north side of Todmorden's Fielden Square, and leads south to Gauxholme where the railway crosses the canal twice within a few hundred yards, on an eighteen-arch stone viaduct and a 101 foot long iron bridge with crenellated abutments. The towpath carries on below and beyond, and just over a mile farther the railway disappears into Summit Tunnel and thence into Lancashire. When built, at one mile and 1,125 yards Summit was the world's longest railway tunnel; George Stephenson thought it was 'the greatest work that has yet been done of this kind'. Road and canal both follow close by the railway to the tunnel entrance and continue together towards the border between the West Riding and Lancashire at Steanor Bottom.

On the junction of the A6033 and a lane at Steanor Bottom stands an early nineteenth century turnpike tollhouse, complete with the original board showing the charges. The pike or gate barred the road, and had to be turned or opened before traffic could proceed. This unusual tollhouse is hexagonal in plan and two storeys high, and fits perfectly into the acute angle formed by the meeting of the two roads.

North-west of Todmorden, the Calder Valley reaches three miles to Cornholme and, just beyond, Lancashire. Across the bleak moorland a mile to the north of this important cross-Pennine route runs the Long Causeway, a packhorse track linking Halifax and Burnley via Hebden Bridge. Most of the causeway is now a by-road, which may be reached by taking the steep and winding lane north out of the Calder Valley from the A646 at Cornholme. This also offers good views across the valley to the south, where the moorland road known as Tower Causeway follows the direct high-level path between Todmorden and Cornholme. The Tower Causeway is accessible from Todmorden via Parkin Lane which runs north then west from opposite the town hall.

Tower Wood, above Cornholme to the south, now boasts no tower but the area has a curious, although probably not unusual, history of illegal gambling. In these secluded hills during the 1920s a group of men, employed at Cornholme bobbin mill, would meet to play at tossing coins on Sunday afternoons. Perhaps twenty millworkers might be involved, sometimes losing a week's wages on a single throw.

Now, as then, the pleasures of the countryside take many forms.

INTO EASTERN EXTREMITIES
The Ouse Basin

Downstream from Goole, the Ouse traverses bleak and marshy flatlands on its journey to the Humber Estuary, while the road on its south bank rolls through a series of villages whose names are redolent of the cold and wet: Swinefleet, Reedness and Ousefleet. In this boggy waste is the most easterly point of the West Riding, a finger of sand protruding into the Humber estuary. Indeed it signifies the start of the estuary, formed by the rivers Wharfe, Derwent, Aire and Don, which join the Ouse before it meets the Trent at this tiny peninsula, Blacktoft Sand just east of Ousefleet.

An embankment path runs east of Whitgift and alongside the sands, taking the walker under vast skies to the middle of nowhere beside the huge estuary. The Ousefleet road continues towards the estuary then turns south through Adlingfleet, Eastoft and back to Goole across the marshland of Goole Fields. Following this route may give the traveller some idea of the conditions facing Dutch engineer Cornelius Vermuyden when he was appointed to drain the area south of Goole in 1626.

The inhabitants of Goole, in the district of Marshland, had for a long time been preoccupied with the battle against flooding. Their settlement, which dates from at least 1362, stood at the junction of a drain (or goul) with the Ouse, and although a system of drainage ditches had been in existence since around 1200, local people had continually found difficulty in maintaining the embankments around their fields.

By the seventeenth century their position had improved to the extent that Vermuyden was invited to try his hand at flood control on a large scale in the Royal Chase of Hatfield, ten miles to the south of Goole, where the Trent and Don sometimes ran amuck. Vermuyden diverted part of the Don but only succeeded in flooding a different area; the solution was found in 1630 when two parallel drains were cut from the Don east to a sluicegate on the Ouse just north of Goole.

Floods in the late seventeenth century swept

One of the locks dividing the River Ouse from Goole Docks.

away the sluice and then the bank between the drains, forming the wide channel still known as the Dutch River (though Vermuyden had departed rapidly after the failure of his engineering works).

Goole remained a tiny agricultural hamlet until well into the nineteenth century,

outstripped in river trade by Selby, the lowest bridging point on the Ouse, and Airmyn, at the junction of Aire and Ouse. Goole's sudden growth began in 1822 with the construction of the Goole Canal, linking the Aire & Calder Navigation at Knottingley with the Ouse. The new canal was needed to take pressure off the

The hand-cranked swing bridge at Goole Docks.

inadequate route from the woollen towns of the Pennines via the lower Aire and the Selby Canal to the sea.

The Goole Canal, which ran just north of the Dutch River on its final stretch, was opened (despite delays caused by drought) on the 20th July 1826. On the great day, coachloads of spectators arrived from all over the West Riding and steam packets brought more trippers to see the massive locks, warehouses and docks. The inevitable festivities included a musical procession of decorated boats. The new port soon became a tourist attraction, and the town expanded to the north of the

Dutch River on a triangular plan drawn up by the navigation's engineer George Leather. Initially New Goole was a boom town, riding on the success of the canal, and architectural style was strictly controlled by the company.

This first spate of growth lasted only ten years, after which competition from Hull and the railways slowed expansion until the second half of the century. The railways reached Goole in the 1840s, despite the efforts of the navigation to stop them, and after improvements to the Ouse below Goole in the 1880s the port began to thrive again. A wave of building began in the 1860s and continued until the First World War, but since then the town's dependence on shipping has brought slow decline, exacerbated by the bridging of the Ouse at Boothferry in 1929 and the coming,

The nautically-inspired ceramic doorcase decoration on the offices of the Goole Steam Shipping Company, built in 1902.

rather later, of the Humber Bridge and the M62. The needs of transport which created the town have now made it almost redundant.

Goole today is an unremarkable small town attached to a memorable and massive complex of docks. Warehouses, cranes, locks and shipping are structured on a giant scale in comparison with the everyday terraces of the townscape. A pair of water towers stands out above the flat landscape: the slender, elegant, red-brick model dates from 1883, while the bowl supported by concrete fretwork was built in 1926-7. The latter was the most capacious water tower in Europe at the time of its construction, holding 750,000 gallons.

The spire near the docks is that of the church of St John, built by the navigation for the town in 1843-8. Its memorials are suitably nautical. The architects of the church were William Hurst and W L Moffatt, who also designed most of the buildings of the new town for the navigation company between 1824 and 1840; these terraces were largely demolished in 1965-6. Moffatt began his architectural career as a pupil of William Burn, while Hurst was initially articled to William Lindley in their home town of Doncaster.

The change from domestic to industrial landscape is sudden: turn a corner from the church and head south towards the river, and immediately a change of scale is apparent. The Ouse itself is vast but the enclosed waters of the docks, little inland seas, are somehow more impressive. Survivors from the port's busier days include the hand-cranked swing bridge in the docks and the boat hoist which lifted coal boats from the water and tipped their contents into ship's holds. The coal boats,

The water towers of 1883 (left) and 1926 at Goole Docks.

known as Tom Puddings, arrived in convoys towed by tugs along the canal from the Yorkshire coalfield.

Away from Goole, a traveller in this land of open spaces will soon discover that the rawness of nature has lost none of its power; rivers bar the way on all sides, and bridges are few and very far between. At Airmyn, two miles from Goole north along the A614 and left before Boothferry Bridge, one can see the neighbouring village of Little Airmyn across the Aire. To reach it involves either a swim or a round trip of fifteen miles via Snaith. Better, perhaps, to stay in Airmyn and admire the spiky Gothic clock tower built in 1865. Airmyn, a river port since medieval times, prospered particularly in the 1770s before the opening of the Selby Canal.

Cross the Aire north of Snaith on the A1041 and press on half a mile into the village of Carlton, dominated by the presence of Carlton Towers, its skyline bursting into view beyond the park gates. Once plain Carlton Hall, the name was changed to reflect the reality of alterations and additions carried out during 1873-5. The house, with its three towers and countless turrets thrusting upward, could have been designed in a game of architectural consequences, but in fact was the work of Edward Welby Pugin, who used the inheritance of Henry Stapleton, the young Lord Beaumont, to produce a palatial Gothic monument to bad taste. Carlton Towers is bulky, big and powerful, but those who fail to appreciate the subtleties of its exterior will be won over by the beautiful interiors.

Part of the house was built in 1614 by Elizabeth Stapleton, great-granddaughter of Bess of Hardwick. A wing, including a chapel, was added in 1777 but soon after 1840 the chapel was removed, as Miles Thomas Stapleton had succeeded in the family claim to the Beaumont title and promptly disposed of his Catholic trappings. Miles died in 1854 and his son Henry came of age in 1869, returning to Catholicism in the same year. He brought in Pugin, of the same faith, to celebrate his fortune and freedom by completely remodelling the existing hall. Large as the house was in 1873, it contained no bathrooms, so perhaps fashion hastened the reconstruction. Pugin covered the old brick façades with grooved concrete in a dull fawn, but created two staircase towers and elaborated on the existing clock tower until it resembled a water tower.

Pugin died in 1875, but John Francis Bentley had already been called in to advise on the interiors. Also a Catholic, he was best known for his work on churches and produced at Carlton a set of brilliant rooms; the Venetian drawing room, with black dado cabinets and lashings of gold almost everywhere else, is especially splendid. Beaumont did not enjoy his plaything for long, as his forays in foreign parts fighting for various causes, combined with financial jousts in the markets, brought the estate into debt by 1879, and Beaumont moved abroad. His brother inherited the house in 1892, and it is now the Yorkshire home of the Duke of Norfolk.

The road north through Carlton takes the driver past more modern towers, those of the Drax power station east of Camblesforth village. Power lines, railway tracks and cooling towers litter the Ouse basin, but the cooling towers at least often add a steamy excitement to the wide skies.

The church of St John
at Goole.

Beyond the power station is Drax itself, where an Augustinian priory was established before 1140. Today nothing remains of this foundation, but the parish church, St Peter and St Paul, has jolly gargoyles on the exterior, and contains fine Norman work as well as a set of mid-fifteenth century carvings of apostles and saints which look down upon the visitor from above the nave arcade.

There is no direct route to Selby from Drax other than walking the Ouse bank, so head north again along the A1041 and the tower of the Norman church of St Wilfrid at Brayton will soon appear, indicating the outskirts of Selby. The road crosses the Selby Canal and deposits the traveller in the market place opposite Selby's main claim to fame, its Benedictine abbey. To equate Selby only with an ancient abbey, however, would be a mistake.

Selby was in its prime during the forty or so years following the opening of the Selby Canal on the 29th April 1778. Work on the canal, which connected the Ouse with the Aire six miles to the south-west, had begun three years before, and opening day saw the usual celebrations with music, cannonfire and bell-ringing. Local people were right to rejoice, as the canal brought prosperity to the town; it already attracted trade from seagoing ships which could progress little further up the Ouse. In 1800 the town handled 369,780 tons of goods and local businesses, many connected with shipping, thrived.

The good times came to an end after the construction of the Goole Canal, although the railway reached Selby from Leeds in 1834 and continued to Hull in 1840, cutting twenty miles off the Selby-Hull journey by river. Today Selby is a country market town which hides its industry beyond the Ouse across the Toll Bridge (the few pence toll was discontinued in September 1991). The bridge was rebuilt in 1970, but the original 1791 structure was probably the earliest wooden bridge in England.

Across the river, gaunt but strangely interesting corn and feed mills line the busy A19, generally ignored by motorists crossing into the West Riding. The combination of bridge, industrial buildings and ancient abbey make Selby stand out in the mind of the traveller desiring no more than to dash along the A19.

Selby Abbey is an oasis in the middle of the town, set amidst greenery and facing the market place but beside the main road. The abbey was founded in 1069, the legend being that Benedict of Auxerre in central France travelled to England as a result of a vision telling him to seek Selebaie. On his way up the Ouse he saw three swans at Selby, which he took as a sign that the abbey should be founded on the site; the present building dates from about 1100. Benedictine communities derived spiritual benefits from their disciplined pattern of communal life, which emphasised worship and work, as opposed to solitary prayer and study.

The abbey was begun by Abbot Hugh de Lacey, and the nave, which took over 100 years to build, shows a progression from Norman to Early English styles and has a fine west doorway. The chancel was built between about 1280 and 1340. The abbey survived the Dissolution intact, only for the central tower to fall in 1690. The south transept was badly damaged, and restoration work was finally carried out in 1871-3 and 1889-90. Fire struck in 1906, affecting the entire abbey, and repairs continued until 1935. Despite these disasters, the abbey retains the atmosphere of structural purity associated with the greatest Norman buildings.

Following the general north-western trend of the Ouse, the B1223 takes the driver rapidly from traffic-strewn Selby to the quiet country around Selby Common and past the door of the white stone All Saints at Wistow, with still not a contour line in sight.

Cawood, on the west bank of the Ouse just over four miles from Selby (doubly as far by river), at first glance is merely another village clustered around a river bridge, but was the site of a great palace in the fourteenth and fifteenth centuries. Romans and Vikings left their mark in Cawood before King Athelstan built a castle here in the tenth century.

In the fourteenth century the castle became the palace of the Archbishop of York; seven archbishops died at Cawood Castle, and in 1466 George Neville celebrated his appointment with an incredible feast at Cawood. Nearly 1,200 servants prepared 2,000 pigs, 1,000 sheep and hundreds and thousands of other beasts; 75,000 gallons of ale washed it all down. Cardinal Wolsey, the Archbishop of York who never visited the town, hoped to make Cawood a palace to rival the Hampton Court of Henry VIII. He employed 300 workmen on the task but to no avail; Wolsey was arrested at Cawood and died soon afterwards, back in the south.

After the Civil War, Cawood was made indefensible, but the gatehouse was used as a courtroom in the eighteenth century. All that remains of Cawood Castle today is the white stone gatehouse built by Archbishop Kempe, in office during 1426-51. This finely-decorated building has two storeys over a double archway, and a pretty oriel window. To either side are brick ranges. It is now in the ownership of the Landmark Trust and used as a holiday cottage.

A mile north of Cawood, the Wharfe takes its leave of the Ouse. Running westward, the Wharfe now forms an unbridged barrier for travellers heading towards York into the forgotten triangle of land between the rivers Ouse and Wharfe, and the main Leeds-York road, the A64.

So continue west along the B1223, through Ryther, where All Saints Church has a weather-boarded bell turret (1898) and the arms of the Ryther family depicted in stained glass in the south window. The glass, with a border of birds and squirrels, dates from about 1325, and as to the fabric of the church, its chancel arch may be late Saxon. The Rythers, an active military family, lived in the village until the mid-sixteenth century.

West of Ulleskelf and almost bordering on the Wharfe is the Grimston Park estate, caught between roads and river. The house was rebuilt by Decimus Burton in 1840 and the Italianate gardens laid out by landscape architect W A Nesfield. It was one of Nesfield's best-known works, with two formal walks, one lined by busts of the twelve Caesars. In the 1920s the sculptures were sold off and the garden abandoned.

A right turn north along the A162 from the Grimston Park junction will take the driver towards Tadcaster and across the Wharfe onto the A64, heading for York. After about six miles take the York road, the A1036, and

The Venetian drawing room at Carlton Towers.

Carlton Towers in the eighteenth century.

then turn right (back over the A64) by a school into Sim Balk Lane and Bishopthorpe. Now, at last, we can begin to explore this curiously inaccessible triangle of land which has Bishopthorpe at its apex.

On the north side of Bishopthorpe, backing on to the Ouse and opposite the church, stands the Archbishop's Palace. The original manor house on the site was given to the Dean and Chapter of York in 1241, predating the palace at Cawood, which in any case was more of a holiday home. A chapel was soon added, then Archbishops Rotherham and Frewen rebuilt much of the property at the end of the fifteenth century and during 1660-4 respectively. The gloriously Gothick façade of the palace was provided by local architect Thomas Atkinson for Archbishop Robert Hay Drummond in 1766-9. Atkinson also designed the gatehouse, on the street frontage, in similar style in 1763-5. His church, St Andrew (1766), was largely demolished in 1899, but the pinnacled west front still stands down a lane beside the palace.

At Acaster Malbis, two miles south by road or riverbank, the church of the Holy Trinity offers a brief history of stained glass, with windows and fragments dating from the fourteenth and fifteenth, nineteenth and twentieth centuries. The best is the earliest, an east window of the mid-fourteenth century showing Christ and the saints, strong in greens and yellows.

Leaving Acaster Malbis, the road meanders south-west across rich agricultural land to Appleton Roebuck and Bolton Percy, where the handsome and spacious All Saints Church (consecrated in 1424) looks out over the peaceful and newly-restored churchyard.

During 1980-92 the one acre cemetery has been transformed from a wilderness to a wildflower garden. The church was designed by its rector, Thomas Parker, who died a year before its completion.

Tadcaster is only a little over three miles west of Bolton Percy, but nothing could be more of a contrast to the rural idyll of the churchyard than the massive breweries which dominate the town on the Wharfe.

This industrial image should not deter the prospective visitor, however, as not only does Tadcaster have a perfectly presentable centre with some very decent Georgian buildings, but the John Smiths Brewery is a fine and spectacular piece of architecture in itself. Indeed the town is one of only three English towns where brewing has such a presence: Alton in Hampshire and the much larger Burton-upon-Trent are the other two, and Tadcaster is unique in squeezing the convivial atmosphere of a northern market town into what could be the Magnet Ales brewery yard.

First, then, to the breweries, drawn here by the high quality of the local supply of hard water. In 1847 the original John Smith bought the High Street brewery at Tadcaster, which had been established in 1758, and took his brother William into partnership. When John died in 1879 he left the brewery to William and a second brother, Samuel, but decreed that the brewery should eventually pass to the heirs of Samuel.

Seeing no long-term future for his family, William Smith built himself a new brewery in 1883, taking the John Smith tradename with him to the new site. Now the tall, golden, Yorkshire stone buildings of John Smith's Tadcaster Brewery dominate the south of the

An architect's perspective of John Smith's Brewery in Tadcaster, 1883.

town, and its elegant polygonal chimney towers over Bridge Street.

The architects of the new brewery were George Scamell and his partner Colyer, a practice from London who specialised in the design of breweries, maltings and the whole complex of allied buildings which went to make up a nineteenth century brewery. They were one of half a dozen such specialist practices, and the chimney of their Tadcaster brewery was one of the last of the great Yorkshire industrial stacks.

Both the Smith breweries thrived, and the black stack south of Bridge Street belongs to Samuel Smith's Old Brewery, a red-brick tower brewery. Brewing on the tower system was introduced in the 1860s, leading to the rebuilding of many breweries in the following

The John Smith's Brewery, Tadcaster.

thirty years. In a tower brewery the ingredients of the brew - basically malt, hops and water - are brought to the top of the tower and then allowed to fall under gravity through the succession of brewing processes. The architectural consequence of this advance in brewing techniques was the construction of numerous handsome tower breweries, which combined the functional repetitions of the warehouse with decorative delights such as the ironwork gates of John Smith's.

Until demolition in 1974 the castellated outline of Tadcaster Tower Brewery made up a trio of tower breweries on the town's skyline, but industrialisation of the brewing trade caught up with the Tower Brewery, and the

Wetherby Road (A659) site, adjacent to the defunct railway line, is now home to the Bass brewery.

Away from the breweries, Tadcaster can boast a railway viaduct never used by a train and a church which was moved in its entirety in 1875-7 to protect it from flooding. The railway station at Tadcaster, on the Harrogate-Church Fenton line, opened in 1847. The 'virgin viaduct' was built two years later across the Wharfe to the north of the bridge, but no railway track was ever laid on this proposed branch line. As to the church of St Mary in Kirkgate, it is Perpendicular in style with a large, white-stone west tower and a multitude of gargoyles. It stands five feet higher than before its rebuilding, and much of its fine stained glass dates from the period immediately after this amazing piece of reconstruction. Look at the east window in particular, with William Morris & Company glass of the late 1870s showing fifteen assorted saints and angels, all set off by exotic joinery in the choir.

Aberford, five miles south-west of Tadcaster, comes as a quiet relief from the high-powered A64 and A1. Eighteenth century houses line the course of the old Great North Road and the Victorian era seems hardly to have touched the village, although the church of St Ricarius was built in 1861 and the most memorable building is also Victorian.

This is the Gascoigne Almshouses, an enormous turreted Gothic construction appended to the south of the village. Its towers rise like a mirage from the west of the main road, making the pretty Gothic lodge look ridiculously tiny. The almshouses were erected in 1844 by the Misses Mary Isabella and Elizabeth Gascoigne of Parlington Hall, a mile south-west of Aberford. The building commemorates their father, Richard Oliver Gascoigne, and their two brothers, all of whom died within a year, and was intended to accommodate eight elderly people who had been tenants on the family estates. The sisters' chosen architect was George Fowler Jones of York, who was aged only twenty-six when he produced this design, his first recorded work. Perhaps he persuaded the good ladies to indulge his taste for intricate stonework.

A bridlepath, Parlington Lane, leads west from Aberford past the remains of Parlington Hall, largely demolished in 1950, towards Garforth. Once away from the village the Triumphal Arch, erected in 1781-3 by Sir Thomas Gascoigne to celebrate American victory in the War of Independence, becomes visible to the north. It was designed by London architect Thomas Leverton; although the victory is an apparently odd subject for an English memorial, at this time Gascoigne would not have been alone in his sympathy with rebellion against the Crown. The Gascoignes owned coalmines in the Garforth area between 1773 and 1920, but the sight of coal wagons passing the hall on the way to Parlington Colliery was too much for Richard Oliver Gascoigne to bear, so in 1813-4 he built the Dark Arch, a tunnel of almost 100 yards which took the wagons, and now the bridlepath, past the hall.

For a trip to the Iron Age, take the Becca Lane bridlepath leading west from the centre of Aberford, opposite the Arabian Horse public house. After escaping the village, the lane runs north-west along the Becca Banks, a phenomenal defensive earthwork constructed by the Brigantes to ward off Roman incursions

The Gascoigne Almshouses, Aberford.

into their northern kingdom of Elmet. The embankment system stretched from the Aire at Swillington, on the south-eastern edge of Leeds beyond Temple Newsam, to Aberford via Barwick in Elmet. The Becca Banks section is two and a half miles long with a ditch which reaches twenty-five feet in depth. The bridlepath follows the Banks for about a mile until the earthworks turn west, running above the line of Cock Beck towards Barwick.

Heading south from Aberford, the traveller passes the pretty pair of Hookmoor Lodges just before the A1 junction at the southern entrance to the Parlington Hall estate.

Four miles further south along the A656 then two miles east is Ledsham, where the Saxon church of All Saints stands proud above the village. Apart from the intrinsic attractiveness of the church, it contains memorials to two remarkable women, Lady Mary Bolles and Lady Elizabeth Hastings.

Mary Bolles, born in 1579, was the daughter of William Witham, the local estate owner, who died when she was aged only fourteen. The death was put down to witchcraft, and indeed Mary Pannal of nearby Ledston was executed for casting the spell. Mary Bolles, who was also rumoured to dabble in magic, spent much of her life at Heath Old Hall, near Wakefield, where she died in 1662. She was granted the title of baroness in her own right in 1635 and distributed her great wealth widely, mainly in charitable bequests but also for a lavish six week wake on the occasion of her death. Elizabeth Hastings owned the Ledston Estate during the early eighteenth century; she built the vicarage, school and orphanage at Ledsham, and continued her charity work until her death in 1740.

All Saints Church, Ledsham.

Travelling east from Aberford, on the by-road south of the church which dips under the A1, in a mile bear left towards Towton on the B1217 and look out for the Crooked Billet Inn at Lead. Take the bridlepath opposite - Chantry Lane - and hop over the stile to visit a tiny chapel which stands alone in a field; this is St Mary's. The eighteen foot long chapel is secluded and tranquil, although it can be unnerving when gusts of wind rattle the door. The simple stonework dates from the fourteenth century, although the joinery is mainly eighteenth century.

The three-decker pulpit at St Mary's, Lead.

Backtrack to the crossroads and head east for Sherburn in Elmet, then take the A162 and A63 further south, into the Vale of York to Monk Fryston; tiny back lanes then lead to the hamlet of Birkin, only a mile north of the Aire. Here, almost on the banks of a small tributary called the Old Eye, stands the impressive grey-stone Norman church of St Mary. It was built around 1160, though a south aisle was added about 1330 and the tower was heightened during the fifteenth century. There is a delightfully-decorated south doorway and a Norman rib-vaulted apse, the only one in the West Riding. East and west of the church, even the presence of so many cooling towers in the middle distance does not diminish one's sense of isolation in this tiny village.

Immediately west of St Mary's, a lane rambles back towards civilisation and the A1 by way of the southern edge of Byram Park estate, a little over two miles from Birkin. 'Capability' Brown advised Sir John Ramsden on the design of the estate in 1782, but the house, decorated by Robert Adam in the 1780s, was demolished around 1922.

The lane joins the A1 opposite Ferrybridge power station; the cooling towers date from 1960, and the distinguished generating hall on the bank of the Aire is also an elegant piece of industrial design. A little further south is the A645 turning for Pontefract, home of the eponymous cake.

Liquorice, a summer-flowering perennial and the main ingredient of Pontefract or Pomfret cakes, once grew within the ruins of Pontefract Castle. The Romans chewed the sweet roots of liquorice, and it was used for medicinal purposes well before 1760 when

The isolated chapel of St Mary at Lead.

George Dunhill, a Pontefract chemist, added sugar and produced the sweet cakes we know today.

The remains of the castle stand on a rocky platform at the north-eastern edge of the town centre. It was built by Ilbert de Lacy in the late eleventh century and figures in history largely as a prison. The castle cells held Richard II until his death - or more probably his murder - in 1400. James I of Scotland was imprisoned at the castle and Charles, Duke of Orleans, was held at Pontefract for many years after his capture at Agincourt. After the surrender of the castle to the Parliamentarians in 1648, the townspeople petitioned that it should be taken down; ten weeks later, only the ruins remained.

The picturesque form of All Saints Church lies close to the castle rock, away from the town centre. It was probably built in the early to mid-fourteenth century, but was so severely damaged during the Civil War that it could no longer be used for worship. In compensation, the town was allowed the money from the sale of the castle building materials, but instead of being put towards the construction of a new church, the money appears to have been embezzled. Some repairs were made to the ruin of All Saints in the seventeenth and nineteenth centuries, and a new church arose inside the original nave in 1967.

The long market place is Pontefract's centre, with the town hall looking over market stalls at St Giles and the Butter Cross. The town hall, a genteel, Classical affair standing on an arcaded base, was built in 1785; its architect was Bernard Hartley I of Pontefract. Hartley was the first of three generations bearing the same name, all of whom held the post of surveyor of bridges to the West Riding. Hartley I was also a bridge designer and something of an inventor; his pile-driving machine, worked by two men and a horse, could do the work of forty men. (The Hartley I influence was spread outside the West Riding by his younger son Jesse Hartley, who was surveyor to the Liverpool Dock Trustees during 1824-60, when he was responsible for the design of the Albert Dock.)

Pontefract market has been held on the site in front of St Giles Church since the twelfth century. The Butter Cross, an open, arcaded, three-bay shelter for market stalls, was built beside the church at the west end of the market place in 1734. It replaced the old market cross, which gave the early market divine protection and acted as its focal point.

In Salter Row, leading from the east end of the market place, stands the library, now the town's museum. Its façade is a striking red-brick and yellow terracotta mixture featuring assorted Art Nouveau motifs; it was built in 1904-5 by architects Garside and George F Pennington.

Before continuing south of Pontefract, seekers of famous names in English architectural history should visit Whitwood, a village on the western fringe of Castleford. The A639 north from Pontefract passes under the M62 and thence through Whitwood, where south of the crossroads are the unmistakable forms of a C F A Voysey design. His work at Whitwood for Briggs Colliery in 1904-5 comprised cottages and an institute (now the Rising Sun pub); the battered (inclined) walls and pale roughcasting give the game away. Voysey was born near Hull (his father was vicar of Healaugh) and is best-known for his country houses, which combined a simplicity of style with elegant detailing. His work at Whitwood is immediately recognisable as a cottage-scale version of a typical Voysey exterior.

Close by is the Whitwood Mere Infants School, designed in 1937-9 by Oliver Hill, the brilliant architect and interior decorator who did much of his best work in the interwar years. His ventures into school design in London and the West Riding were constantly frustrated by forces beyond his control; only at Whitwood did his efforts, given free of charge, come to fruition. Whitwood was an attempt to bring light and air to children in a colliery area - thus the long curve of classrooms with windows facing south. The windows folded back completely to let in the sun. The complementary curve of the broad canopy which shades an outdoor play area is reminiscent of many a seaside pavilion. Strange that Whitwood should attract two such individualistic twentieth century architects, but perhaps it is simply a reflection of the progressive nature of local employers.

Leave Pontefract by the A628, which passes through Ackworth. Here we find further evidence of social progressiveness at the Friends' school, originally the Foundling Hospital of 1758-65, but bought by the Society of Friends in 1778 and opened in 1779 as a school for the children of poor Quakers. The school was designed on the country house pattern of a central block with side wings; in this case the connection between the two is made by delightful (if eroded) curving Tuscan colonnades.

At Ackworth Moor Top, turn right along the A638 towards Wakefield; the main gates of Nostell Park, the estate of the Palladian mansion Nostell Priory, soon appear to the right.

The Augustinian priory of that name was founded in 1121 by Ralph Adlave, chaplain to Henry I, on a site already occupied by a small colony of monks belonging to a Saxon order. A church and monastic buildings were erected during the twelfth century and the priory became a sizeable and busy concern; by the thirteenth century, three servants were employed for every canon at Nostell. After suppression of the monastery in 1540 the estate, now substantial, passed through various hands, being sold to the Winn family of London merchants in 1650.

Previous owners lived in a house converted from part of the priory church (south-west of the present house), and the Winns followed suit until the coming of the fourth baronet, Sir Rowland Winn. His lengthy grand tour of Europe around 1722-7 imbued him with fashionable architectural ideas, and marriage to an heiress in 1729 gave him the means to build anew. Sir Rowland moved in artistic circles, and it seems that his acquaintances included Colonel James Moyser, a Yorkshire amateur architect who helped with the design of Bretton Hall, six miles north-west of Barnsley, around 1720.

Moyser was responsible for the original plan of Nostell Priory, although it was implemented and modified by the young James Paine from 1736. The design, a thirteen-bay main block with four connected pavilions, was still being built in 1765 when Sir Rowland died, and was never completely finished.

The fifth baronet, also Sir Rowland, asked the newly-fashionable Robert Adam to continue work on the house; the result was a sequence of Adam interiors dating from 1766-76 which combine with Paine's Rococo decoration to show the changes in English taste between the 1740s and the 1760s. Complementary to these exquisite rooms is a fine collection of Chippendale furniture. Thomas Chippendale, born in Otley, furnished the entire house for Sir Rowland during 1766-76, supplying everything from expensive, carved cabinets to a kitchen chopping-block. Adam added the family wing to the north-east of the main, pedimented block in 1779-80 (it was only completed in 1875), and the stables date from 1827-9.

Of course, the magnificent new house needed a worthy setting, and plans for the redesign of Nostell Park were being drawn up even before a start was made on construction of the priory. The fourth baronet called in Stephen Switzer, a garden designer and seedsman who worked at Castle Howard in the 1720s, to produce a plan for the park around 1734. Switzer had to take in two important existing features, the natural lake and the church of St Michael and Our Lady - Wragby parish church - which stands just inside the main gates.

The chancel of St Michael, if not the entire church, was built for the penultimate prior at Nostell Priory in 1533. There are monuments to the fourth baronet and John Winn, who died in Rome in 1817. John Winn brought to the church 489 panels of Swiss glass, dating from 1514 to 1745, collected on his tours of Europe. The glass, now removed, took up all but two of St Michael's nineteen windows.

Switzer suggested siting a group of features around the central lake, and made no great distinction between garden and park. Little of Switzer's work is visible except the dam at the northern end of the natural lake (just west of the house). A stream leads from the dam to the lower lake. Adam, not content with his alterations to the priory, left his mark on the park with the lodge and gates at Foulby (1777-8), a mile west of the main gates on the A638, and the peculiar Pyramid Lodge (1776) on Featherstone Moor at the now little-used north entrance to the park.

The Pyramid Lodge, also known as the Needle's Eye, is in the form of a huge stone pyramid cut through by an archway wide enough to take a carriage. Abutting on either side are small lodge houses, their chimney flues running within the pyramid. The walk of a mile or so from the main gates and Wragby Church, via the splendid façade of Nostell Priory and north past the lake down to the perturbing pyramid, encompasses the history of the estate and the changing face of English neo-Classical architecture.

DEFACED TO THE UTTERMOST

Dearne and Don

The south-eastern corner of the West Riding is much misunderstood. It is generally regarded as scenic wallpaper by those in transit by car or train who cannot be persuaded to explore the hidden delights of the Yorkshire coalfield.

Certainly the area is cut about by motorways, railways and the remnants of canals, and evidence of coalmining is often obtrusive, but between the flat lands of Thorne Waste in the east and the Pennine foothills in the west are not only motorway services but magnificent follies, a modern pleasure dome, the longest country house front in England and one of the tallest structures in Europe.

First to the south, where the crossing of the M18 and the A1(M) defines a quiet triangle of land edged by motorways, which extends to the border with Derbyshire and Nottinghamshire. Two miles south of Maltby, in the bottom of a secluded valley off the A634, are the ruins of Roche Abbey.

Although the east end of the church is still standing, and excavation has made the lay-out of the site easy to comprehend, the beauty of Roche Abbey lies in its setting. White magnesian limestone cliffs approach the church to its north, and trees almost surround the narrow, grassy valley. A stream, Maltby Dike, which runs east via the waters of the Idle and the Ryton into the Trent, passes under the remains of the monks' dormitory (dorter) and refectory (frater). The stream, cleaner today, functioned as the monastery drain. The Cistercian abbey of St Mary of Roche was founded in 1147, and by the end of the twelfth century probably accommodated about eighty monks and lay brothers. The church was complete by 1160-70, and its pointed arches show signs of Gothic development, in which massive forms were slowly replaced by minimalist structures giving a greater sense of space. The monastic buildings, visible now in outline only, represent a typical late twelfth century Cistercian plan.

Roche slowly declined over the centuries until the Dissolution, and only the abbot and eighteen monks remained to surrender to the Crown on the 23rd June 1538. Local people immediately plundered the site for building materials, and a contemporary account reports the abbey as being 'defaced to the uttermost'.

In 1544 the remnants of the abbey with its lands were granted to Thomas Vavasour and William Ramsden, and after several changes of ownership came into the hands of the earls of Scarbrough during the eighteenth century. Sandbeck Park, a couple of miles east of the abbey, was also part of the Scarbrough estate; the Sandbeck Park mansion was remodelled for the fourth earl by James Paine around 1763-8. Roche Abbey fitted perfectly into Sandbeck Park as an elegant ruin, and Lancelot 'Capability' Brown landscaped the park, including the abbey grounds, in 1766. This was two years before William Aislabie managed to buy the Fountains estate and secure his own picturesque view.

South of the abbey are several pretty villages. Just over a mile east along the A634 is the turning for Firbeck, once dominated by the St Leger estate of Park Hill. The St Leger family, of horse-race fame, moved to Park Hill around 1765, but their home, on the south side of Firbeck, was demolished in 1935. They built ornate estate cottages on the main village street in 1876. A mile further south is Lethwell, where an octagonal dovecote stands to the south of the village street. The two-storey red-brick building probably dates from the late eighteenth century; inside, tiers of nesting holes are reached by a ladder which revolves around a central post.

Two miles south-west of Roche Abbey at Laughton-en-le-Maughton, the Gothic spire of All Saints Church reaches upward with the aid of two sets of flying buttresses, one above the other. This delicate construction rises from a church which is mainly Anglo-Saxon and Norman, and stands next to Castle Hill, once the site of a motte and bailey castle. The motte or mound was topped by a tower within a court or bailey.

Much more Norman work is on display at the church of St Peter in the village of Thorpe Salvin, six miles south through heavily-developed North and South Anston, and only a mile or so from the county boundary. The font in particular, cylindrical and peopled by jolly sculptured figures, is curious.

On the way to Thorpe Salvin, the traveller heading out of South Anston on the B6059 will pass Kiveton Park to the west, where the first Duke of Leeds built his mansion in 1698-1704. William Talman, popular Whig country house architect and great rival of Christopher Wren, drew up plans for the house but seems not to have gained the commission; perhaps Talman's frequent arguments with clients dissuaded the duke. The mansion lasted only a little over a century before it was demolished in 1811.

The Chesterfield Canal, another relic of the eighteenth century, runs to the south of Kiveton Park. It connected Chesterfield with Worksop and the Trent. Its valley course is now shared by the railway, and the Thorpe Salvin road crosses canal and rails at Kiveton Park Station. Half a mile west, the canal disappears into the hillside at the start of Norwood Tunnel and almost two miles later emerges in the Rother Valley.

Four miles north-east of Roche Abbey as the crow flies is Tickhill and the remains of its famous castle; the A631 passes between the castle mount and the huge parish church of St Mary, with its 124 foot tower.

Medieval Tickhill was an important market centre, the second largest town in south Yorkshire in the mid-fourteenth century, but its decline began in the fifteenth century. The castle originated in Norman times; its gatehouse was added around 1140 and Henry II built an eleven-sided keep on the seventy-five foot high mount in 1178-9. Most of the curtain wall, dating from about 1180, still stands but Parliamentarians destroyed the keep and only the foundations remain.

Rather than rushing northward to Doncaster, a diversion east into the Trent basin produces some small but acceptable pleasures. The A631 leads on to Bawtry, a Norman new town which rapidly developed into a busy market and manufacturing centre. Its wide market place is Georgian in character, with several coaching inns answering demand from traffic on the Great North Road.

Follow the A614 a mile or so north to Austerfield, birthplace of William Bradford, one of the Pilgrim Fathers and second governor of Massachusetts. He was born in 1590 and sailed to America on the *Mayflower* thirty years later. He was baptised in the village church of St Helen, a largely Norman structure with a carved dragon on guard above the south doorway. What must Bradford, eventually an extreme Puritan, have thought of the beckoning sheila-na-gig (fertility figure) looking down on the congregation from a capital in the north aisle?

Press on north via the A614 and turn left to Hatfield on the A18. The main road skirts the village, so bear right at the church of St Lawrence with its dominant Tudor crossing tower. From the church, head north-west for Stainforth and then Fishlake, which lies across the Don in the wet lowlands. (Windmills are never far away.) Hidden in this tiny village is a fine church, St Cuthbert, with an excellent decorated Norman south doorway. Here are virtues fighting vices, and assorted humans and animals, all in four orders of columns.

West of Fishlake, a country lane crosses the New Junction Canal on its way to Moss. The New Junction is that rarity, a twentieth century canal. It was opened on the 2nd January 1905 and connected the Aire & Calder Navigation with the Don Navigation north of Doncaster. The five and a half mile straight cut with a single lock cost £300,000.

From Moss, cross the A19 at Askern and continue to Campsall, apocryphal base for Robin Hood while playing havoc with travellers in the surrounding Barnsdale Forest. Another fugitive resides in the south transept of St Mary Magdalene: the altar from Ackworth Grange, seven miles distant (on the way to Nostell Priory). The grange, demolished in the 1960s, was late Georgian but its chapel was designed by A W N Pugin in 1842. His carved and painted stone altar now ornaments Campsall Church, with its outstanding Norman tower.

The lane south-west from Campsall joins the A19, which will take the driver into Doncaster.

Soon after meeting the trunk road, look out for four Doric columns fronting the white lodge house of Owston Hall to the west. The lodge was built around 1820, and the hall, well away from the road, was designed by William Lindley of Doncaster and erected in 1794-5. Lindley worked as an assistant to

St Mary Magdalene, Campsall.

John Carr for over twenty years before setting up on his own account.

Six miles south are the pleasure domes of Doncaster. The town's origins go back to Roman times when it was a bridging point on the Don and the site of the Roman camp of Danum, which had sizeable iron and pottery works. It had a substantial market, and agriculture was for many centuries the source of Doncaster's wealth, even after the opening of the canal in the 1730s. The River Don Navigation runs close by the river itself on the western edge of the town.

The commercial focus changed dramatically from agriculture to industry with the arrival of the railway in 1848 and then, crucially, the

Great Northern Railway engineering works. In 1853 the Great Northern moved its repair shops and their 900 employees from Boston to a site on the fringe of Doncaster, to the south-west of the station. By 1871 the population of the town had risen to almost 19,000.

The importance of Doncaster as a commercial centre resulted in a building boom towards the end of the nineteenth century, with acres of brick-built terraces filling the low-lying area east of the river and much rebuilding in the town centre. Although much of this new housing lacked originality, an exception is Brunswick Villas on Balby Road (A630) leading west from Doncaster, about a mile from the centre. The builder of these turn of the century three-storey houses chose to decorate the porches with an array of colourful tiles - perhaps a manufacturer's job lot? - which include high-relief tiles of pears so plump they seem ready to pluck.

The Mansion House in High Street is the most noteworthy of Doncaster's (relatively) early buildings, dating from 1745-8. Its original architect was James Paine, who designed the elegant ballroom behind the first floor façade of Corinthian columns, but William Lindley was responsible for the addition of a third storey in 1800-1 and a new banqueting hall in 1806.

The market hall, a complex structure dating from three separate building periods, dominates the market place, with a top-lit hall resembling a station trainshed. The original market hall was built by Doncaster corporation architect J Butterfield in 1847-9, then William Watkins designed the adjacent corn exchange in 1870-3 and a fish market was added in 1930.

Doncaster's parish church of St George.

The interior of the hall can be gloomy but has some elegant decorative ironwork.

The massive parish church of St George was built by George Gilbert Scott in 1854-8 to replace its medieval predecessor, burnt out in 1853. At the time of the fire Doncaster had no telegraph service, so the mayor persuaded the South Yorkshire Railway to run a train to

Swinton, near Rotherham, where a telegraph message could be sent to Sheffield requesting help. But it was all to no avail.

Scott's cathedral-like church is around 170 feet long and the crossing tower stands 170 feet high; the vaulted crypt of the first St George is still intact, and lies below the vestry. Although a fine church, it is cut off from the centre by the ring road and a particularly seedy subway, making it almost irrelevant to the town.

Doncaster has been connected with sporting entertainment since horse races were first held in the town in 1595. The St Leger, one of the five great classics of the English flat racing season, was first run at Doncaster in 1776 on the Cantley Common course, although the event was not known as the St Leger until

An 1832 engraving of John Carr's grandstand at Doncaster racecourse, built in 1777-81.

The church of St Mary Magdalene, Campsall, with its outstanding Norman tower.

Tilework in the porch of Brunswick Villas, Balby Road, Doncaster.

1778 when racing was transferred to Town Moor, where it has taken place ever since. The race was named after Lieutenant-Colonel Anthony St Leger of Park Hill, about ten miles south of Doncaster.

The first grandstand at the racecourse was built in 1777-81 by John Carr. Carr made his name with a grandstand designed for Knavesmire racecourse at York in 1755-6, and built a stand at Nottingham racecourse in 1777. Carr's Doncaster stand had an array of arched windows and broad, bowed ends; when crowded it resembled the lower tiers of a wedding cake. It was demolished in 1968, and of his three grandstand designs, only a part of the York building survives. The Noblemen's Stand, a frilly mixture of cast iron columns and balconies, was added to Doncaster racecourse in 1826, and the Ladies Stand in 1851. Both were also demolished in 1968, but the yellow-brick second enclosure stand, built in 1881 and extended in 1901, is still in use.

Additional spectator accommodation was required as the four-day September St Leger meeting developed from a select event into a mass entertainment towards the end of the nineteenth century.

In 1888 the Great Northern Railway transported nearly 100,000 racegoers to the meeting, and although goods traffic was suspended on St Leger day, all main-line services through Doncaster continued uninterrupted and on time. During the Second World War the St Leger was run at other Northern courses; when it returned to Doncaster in 1946 the common was besieged by a crowd of 140,000.

Directly across the A638 from the racecourse is the Dome, Doncaster's latest offering to pleasure seekers. It is a gloriously striped and domed leisure centre built in 1986-9 for Doncaster Council by FaulknerBrowns of Newcastle-upon-Tyne, specialists in hi-tech leisure centre design. The monster pleasure-palace cost £19,000,000 and is intended not only to serve local people but to stimulate new development in the town.

Certainly it creates wonderful images: from its totally unexpected appearance on the edge of Doncaster to its interior, which combines the latest technology with Classical motifs, the Dome radiates fun. Visitors may wander freely into to the glazed forum, a striped temple to hedonism which is the Dome's centre point.

Take the ten minute train ride from Doncaster, upstream along the Don through gritty industrial landscape to Conisbrough, where two outstanding structures are less than a mile but more than seven centuries apart. As the train crosses the Don on its approach to Conisbrough, passengers are treated to a fine view of Conisbrough Viaduct, opened in 1907 by the Dearne Valley Railway, a coal carrier. The viaduct was the last of this heroic size to be built in Britain. It has twenty-one arches in its 508 yard length and was constructed from blue engineering brick, stronger than everyday red brick. The steel span across the river runs 113 feet above the water.

The present-day line then passes under the old railway to reveal the perfect lines of the towering circular keep of Conisbrough Castle on the far bank of the Don. The creamy whiteness of the smooth stone, the position of the keep above the river guarding the end of a steep valley, the pure geometry of its shape and the odd juxtaposition of a twelfth century castle and the remains of modern industry conspire to make the castle a magnificent monument.

The castle was built by the de Warenne family; William I, the Conquerer, gave William de Warenne a whole collection of estates and castles, three in the south as well as Conisbrough and at least two more in Yorkshire. In 1163 the Conisbrough lands passed, through marriage, to Hameline Plantagenet, a half brother of Henry II. Plantagenet took his wife's family name and proceeded to build matching keeps at Conisbrough and on his estate in Normandy.

The Conisbrough keep probably dates from around 1180. It is ninety feet high and is supported by six massive buttresses, each nine feet thick. Apart from adding to the elegance of the structural geometry, the buttress-top platforms allowed defenders an unimpeded view of the castle walls. A chapel built into the south-east buttress was used by Sir Walter Scott as the setting for a scene in *Ivanhoe*; he described the room as 'small and very rude'. In other buttresses are a dovecote and, less romantically, cisterns and an oven.

Nearby in Conisbrough town, the church of St Peter is home to a unique Norman tomb-chest or stone coffin. The top and sides of this funeral monument are packed with carved decoration - wild scenes including a curly-tailed dragon battling with a human, Adam and Eve, and the signs of the zodiac.

Just upstream from the centre of Conisbrough, the River Dearne enters the Don at the end of its wriggling course from Barnsley and beyond in the north-west. The A635 Doncaster-Barnsley road enjoys a fairly rural ride at least as far as Hickleton village, where James Paine built Hickleton Hall for Godfrey Wentworth in 1745-8. It was one of Paine's earliest country houses, a solid seven-bay pedimented block, which was later enlarged and is now a Sue Ryder home with fine gardens.

The church of St Wilfrid, begun in the twelfth century and completed in the fifteenth, was restored in 1876-88 by George Frederick Bodley, a pupil of George Gilbert Scott. The colourful chancel is typical of his highly-decorative Gothic style, and a bust of the

St Wilfrid's Church, Hickleton.

architect adorns the lady chapel; massive memorials to the various viscounts Halifax dominate the south chapel. Visitors entering the churchyard by the north-west lychgate are greeted by three skulls set into the archway, bearing the message 'Today for me, tomorrow for thee'.

The Dome, Doncaster Leisure Park.

The south chapel and chancel of Hickleton Church.

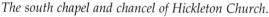

The bust of architect G F Bodley in the lady chapel of Hickleton Church.

Only two miles north of Hickleton, along the lane running north at the crossroads, is the village of Brodsworth, where the church of St Michael and All Angels stands on a wooded hill above the village. The path winds up the hill from the main street, passing above massive walled gardens and leading into the churchyard. The church is partly Norman and partly thirteenth century, with a south aisle added in 1874. Jolly gargoyles ornament the tower of this quiet and secluded little church. A hefty claw-footed tomb guards the path from the churchyard to Brodsworth Hall, currently under restoration.

The hall, in Italian-influenced Classical style, was built by an unknown Italian

St Michael and All Angels, Brodsworth.

architect, Chevalier Casentini from Lucca, in 1861-3. His client was Charles Sabine Thellusson, great-grandson and heir of banker Peter Thellusson, who died in 1797 leaving a complex will; many years of litigation were required to unravel rival claims. Charles Sabine Thellusson finally inherited Brodsworth Hall, a Georgian house, in 1859; he demolished it almost immediately and began building anew. Thellusson's enthusiasm for Italian sculpture probably led to the employment of an Italian architect. Casentini never visited England, and an obscure London architect, Philip Wilkinson, actually carried out the plans.

Brodsworth's thirteen-bay cream stone façade is topped by urns on a balustrade. The hall and gardens are exceptional as they remain little changed by human hand since the 1860s, although natural growth has obscured the original garden plan. The hall was richly-decorated and packed with Italian sculpture. Formal gardens existed near the house, and these are being recreated on their former plan, with the park to follow. Most exciting of all is the quarry garden west of the hall, wild and romantic with paths climbing around rocks and rockeries, lined by ivy hanging from decorative iron supports.

Hooton Pagnell, two miles west of Brodsworth on the B6422, is as picturesque as any Cotswold village and rather quieter. Sinuous streets take the traveller past the daunting gatehouse of Hooton Pagnell Hall, the largely Norman church of All Saints, and assorted stone-built and flower-strewn

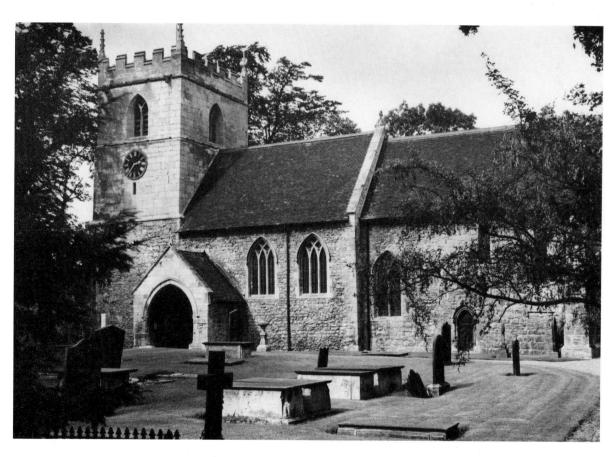

All Saints, Hooton Pagnell, is largely Norman.

cottages. The hall gatehouse originated in the fourteenth century but was much rebuilt in the nineteenth, adding to the military effect. The village occupies a hillside and the view to the west from its main street, over cottage roofs and tiers of gardens, is expansive and happily rural.

Back on the A635 at Hickleton, head west for Barnsley, but before dashing straight into the town centre, turn right (on to the A633) at the Stairfoot roundabout on the outskirts of town to find Monk Bretton Priory.

Although the priory is on the banks of the Dearne, visitors will need to suspend disbelief in the setting of power lines, sewage works, old railway tracks and a housing estate. But walking among the red sandstone ruins is peaceful, and connoisseurs of monastic life may inspect a particularly well-preserved drainage system.

The Priory of St Mary Magdalene of Monk Bretton was founded about 1154 by Adam Fitzswane, whose father was a benefactor of the Cluniac house at Pontefract. Both Pontefract and the new foundation claimed the right to choose Monk Bretton's prior, and the dispute between the houses continued for over a century, with appeals to the pope and Edward I, and even an armed confrontation. In 1281 Monk Bretton went its own way as an independent Benedictine house, preferring a rather more worldly existence to the elaborate liturgy of Cluny.

The priory church was begun in the late twelfth century but later extended, and most of the monastic buildings date from the thirteenth century. Site drainage was regulated by a small sluice gate under the kitchen yard, which allowed the water to be held back during dry periods so that a sudden release would ensure a good flow through the rere-dorter (lavatory). Although the Dissolution brought monastic life at Monk Bretton to an end in 1538, the unusually zealous monks purchased 148 books from the Monk Bretton library at the auction of priory property and transferred their community to Worsborough, on the southern edge of Barnsley, where they stayed for at least twenty years. The priory was stripped of building materials and used as a family home; after many changes of ownership, Barnsley Council bought the site around 1930. Priory Mill, the former monastic corn mill, has recently been converted into a public house.

For a good view over Barnsley, leave the priory by crossing back over the Dearne and turn right at the roundabout; keep south of the town centre, heading for Dodworth along the A6133, and look for Locke Park and its tower to the left.

The hillside provides a prospect of Barnsley, centre of the Yorkshire coalfield, but known as a coal town only since the start of the nineteenth century. However, its history as a market town began in 1249 or posibly even earlier. Barnsley was a major producer of flax and linen before the mid-nineteenth century, eventually becoming the centre of linen powerloom weaving, which was introduced from the mid-1830s. Despite the increasing number of powerlooms, there were still over 1,100 linen handloom weavers in Barnsley in 1871. Both textiles and the iron trade, which provided raw material for comb and needle making, were cottage-based.

The thick Barnsley coal seam was mined for local consumption during the eighteenth century, but by 1800 coal was in great demand from further afield, and the town expanded rapidly during the nineteenth century as mining prospered and transport links improved. Early pits were to the west of Barnsley where the seam was near the surface, but improved techniques led to deeper shafts being dug at pits east of Barnsley, where the dip of the strata took the coal measures below the magnesian limestone. Coal brought jobs and wealth, but also dangers: a mile east of Locke Park on Kendray Hill stands an obelisk and statue, commemorating 361 men and boys who died in an underground explosion at the Old Oaks colliery in 1866.

Locke Park was given to the people of Barnsley in 1861 by Phoebe Locke in memory of her husband, railway engineer Joseph Locke, who was educated at Barnsley Grammar School. As well as being one of the leading civil engineers of his day, Locke was an astute and successful businessman. He specialised in constructing railways with a minimum of tunnels and viaducts; these were cheap to build but could be steep and circuitous, thus expensive to run. He died in 1860 at the age of fifty-five, and is best known for his work on the London-Scotland route via Shap, although he worked on many lines in Britain and Europe. Phoebe Locke died in 1866 and in 1877 her sister, Miss McCreary, put up the Locke Park Tower in her memory.

Barnsley's most outstanding building, its tall tower visible from the M1 and for miles around, is the town hall, built in 1932-3 in Portland stone using a robust Classical revival style.

West of Barnsley, hidden in the undulating wooded hills between the Dearne and Don valleys, is an astounding collection of country houses and accompanying follies, several of them the product of rivalry beween branches of the Wentworth family.

First to Wentworth Castle, three miles south-west of Barnsley: from Locke Park, follow the A6133 then the B6099 west towards Dodworth, turning left immediately after crossing the motorway. A right turn at the T-junction takes driver past the entrance to Wentworth Castle and close by Stainborough Castle. Alternatively a left turn leads south through Birdwell, then via the A6135 and B6090 to Wentworth village, Wentworth Park and the Wentworth seat, Wentworth Wood-house. Only seven miles separate these competing mansions, whose history is indivisible.

The first of the Wentworths to come to prominence was Thomas Wentworth (1593-1641), who succeeded to the Wentworth estate in 1614 and built the first Wentworth Woodhouse around 1630. He was created Baron Raby and Earl of Strafford in 1640, and was the chief minister to Charles I. He was Lord Deputy of Ireland, but the Long Parliament demanded his recall, and after a trial concerned with his responsibility for the upsurge in Irish catholicism, he was executed at the Tower of London on the 24th May 1641. His memorial may be found in Holy Trinity Church at Wentworth village, just east of Wentworth Woodhouse. The second earl died in 1695, leaving the estate to his nephew Thomas Watson, although the title of Lord Raby passed to the first earl's great-nephew Thomas Wentworth (1672-1739).

Lord Raby, a soldier and Tory diplomat, thus had a title but no means of outwardly expressing his status, an intolerable position at a time when a man was judged by the quality of his house and estates. To resolve this he bought the Stainborough estate in 1708 and built himself a grand mansion, which became known as Wentworth Castle.

A house built around 1670 already occupied the site, and Raby immediately added a palatial block, the east range, in a refined French Baroque style. Raby was ambassador to Berlin during 1703-11, where he met the French general and military engineer, Jean de Bodt. Although the general seems never to have visited Wentworth, he was responsible for the design of the new house. The interior of the east range was of the required magnificence, and Raby's rise to respectability (and parity with Watson at Wentworth Woodhouse), was completed in 1711 when the earldom of Strafford was revived and he became first earl of its second creation.

But Strafford had hardly begun building. On a hill half a mile west of his new home he put up a sham castle in the early 1730s which he called Stainborough Castle. One of its four corner towers remains intact, as does Steeple Lodge, a fake Gothick church dating from 1734 which stands near the main gates.

The second earl, William Wentworth, inherited in 1739, and proceeded to dot the park and surrounding countryside with all manner of follies, including an obelisk, a Chinese temple, a sham fort and a pyramid, all in the latest architectural forms of good taste. Most have disappeared, but to the east of the castle, close by the Birdwell road, is an obelisk dedicated to Lady Mary Wortley Montagu, a neighbour who introduced smallpox inoculation to Britain in 1720.

It is no surprise to find that this elongated bout of architectural ostentation provoked a response in kind from Wentworth Woodhouse. Thomas Watson, inheritor of the estate and distant relative of Lord Raby, died in 1723 having given Wentworth Woodhouse to his son Thomas Watson Wentworth (1693-1750) in 1716.

The young Wentworth was an ambitious Whig member of parliament, keen to earn promotion from prime minister Sir Robert Walpole, who was dealing with the aftermath of the South Sea Bubble scandal. Wentworth felt he could be useful to the government and influential with local voters in Yorkshire, so promptly set about bringing Wentworth Woodhouse up to the standard expected of a man of power. First, in 1725-34, he added a west range to the seventeenth century house. Its red-brick and sandstone façade was designed in a decorative, rather foreign Baroque style by an unknown architect.

As building work at Wentworth Woodhouse progressed, its owner's political aspirations slowly came to fulfilment. He was knighted in 1725, rewarded with a barony in 1728 and created Lord Malton in 1733. Neither honours nor house satisfied his ambition, and before the west range was even complete a start had been made on the east range, a wholly separate house.

It is a vast Palladian edifice, its façade at 606 feet the longest country house front in England, and was not finished until around 1770. The architect was first Ralph Tunnicliffe of Rotherham, who died in 1736, and then Henry Flitcroft, a carpenter who became assistant to Lord Burlington and an architect in his own right. Flitcroft revised the original plan for the east range; his Palladian schemes suited the landowning gentry, and made impressive shows of wealth and power.

The interiors of Wentworth Woodhouse, contained in this peculiar back-to-back structure of two distinct houses, encompass changes of taste during only a single generation but stretch from the jolly Rococo of the west entrance hall to the cool Classical perfection of the marble saloon - the main showpiece room of the house. It is sixty feet square, lined with Ionic columns at its lower level and pilasters above a gallery. The marble saloon is placed centrally on the first floor of the east front, and could originally be entered internally via the grand staircase (added in the 1770s by John Carr) or externally from twin flights of stairs meeting under the portico. The marble saloon is supported by the Doric columns of the pillared hall; its large fireplaces and low ceiling give it a surprisingly homely atmosphere.

The rise of Thomas Watson Wentworth continued. On the death of a cousin in 1746 he became Baron Rockingham, and within two months was created the Marquess of Rockingham. His pleasure at this honour had, of course, to be shown through building and he engaged Flitcroft to design a fitting monument, a gesture of thanks turned to stone.

Flitcroft produced one of the strangest follies in England, the Hoober Stand, a tapering triangular tower topped by a cupola, the whole reaching ninety feet in height. The 'stand' (a local name for a tower) rises above the village of Hoober, which is on the B6090 just over a mile east of Wentworth. The tower is sited beside a small lane, a little north-west of the village. Its stone is now blackened, making it a curiously chilling folly. Hoober Stand was completed in 1748 and probably cost Wentworth about £3,000.

Charles, second Marquess of Rockingham (1730-82), succeeded his father in 1750 and rose to the ultimate political height of prime minister in 1765-6 and again in 1782, leading the Whig opposition in between. He found time to add one glorious folly to the Wentworth Woodhouse estate, Keppel's Column in 1776-81, and is often credited with building another, the Needle's Eye.

Keppel's monument is almost in Rotherham: from Wentworth village, take the road south which zig-zags through Scholes, then turn left at the A629 and the edifice is on the left (it is only a mile or so along the A629 east of junction 35 on the M1). The huge Tuscan column, 115 feet in height, was built by John Carr in honour of Viscount Keppel, Rockingham's friend and First Lord of the Admiralty; he was acquitted at a court martial on a charge of cowardice arising from an engagement with the French at Brest in 1778. The column project was begun in 1773 and underwent several changes.

The Needle's Eye is hidden away in Lee Wood, on a hill at the end of Street Lane, nearly a mile to the north of the house. It is a tall stone pyramid pierced by an ogee arch (one pointed at its head) and topped by a large and ludicrous urn. Its designer is unknown, and the story goes that it was built to enable Rockingham to win a bet that he could drive a carriage through the eye of a needle. Indeed the second marquess was a keen horse-racing man and the owner of Whistlejacket, the stallion painted by Stubbs, so this has a ring of truth, but documentary evidence suggests that the Needle's Eye was built between 1722 and 1733, and that Rockingham's involvement is just a pleasant fairy tale.

After Rockingham's death in 1782 his body was placed in the Rockingham Mausoleum, a three-tiered tower with four outlying obelisks, sited on the estate near Nether Haugh. It was designed by Carr in 1785-91 for Rockingham's heir, Charles, fourth Earl Fitzwilliam.

The Fitzwilliams were later involved with coalmining, through entrepreneurs who worked mines on the estate, and the ceramic industry, by way of the Swinton Pottery. In 1806-20 the Fitzwilliam family made extensive loans to the Bramelds, who owned the pottery, and eventually the earl became its sole mortgagee. The pottery was renamed the Rockingham Pottery in 1826 and the griffin from the family crest was used as a factory identification mark. Despite the production of elegant Red Griffin ware and Puce Griffin porcelain, the works closed in 1841. A red-brick bottle kiln survives on the site of the works, on the west of Blackamoor Road (the B6092), which takes the traveller directly from Wentworth into Swinton.

Twelve miles north along the M1 from Wentworth Woodhouse are two more Wentworth country houses, Woolley Hall and Bretton Hall, east and west respectively of junction 38. Woolley, on the hillside below Woolley Edge, was rebuilt in the 1630s by Michael Wentworth, kinsman of Strafford, who had bought the manor of Woolley in 1599.

Bretton was designed by its owner, Sir William Wentworth, with the help of amateur architect Colonel James Moyser around 1720. Sir William was a cousin of Lord Raby and had spent the years 1709 to 1712 on a grand tour of Europe. The house is a plain Classical box, improved by the addition of a bow front and portico in 1811-14. The grounds were landscaped and two lakes introduced by means of damming the Dearne. This work probably took place in the 1760s, and now makes a wonderful setting for the Yorkshire Sculpture Park.

Upstream from Bretton, the Dearne flows along the southern edge of Emley Moor. From the A636 west of Bretton, take the road through Emley village to cross the moor at its highest point, 866 feet above sea level, and find a modern structure, the Emley Moor Mast, which might be admired by the Wentworths of soaring architectural ambition.

The television mast stands over 1,000 feet high and is one of the tallest structures in Europe. It has a fine site, an elegant design, is well-engineered and is an expression of power; in fact, it has all the main attributes of an eighteenth century country house.

TUNNEL AND TORRENT

Sheffield and the South Pennines

On the 4th April 1811 a party of around 500 people disappeared into a hole in the hillside at Diggle, to the north-east of Oldham, watched by 10,000 spectators and accompanied by the strains of *Rule Britannia*. An hour and forty minutes later the party emerged into the daylight at Marsden, just over three miles farther north-east. After seventeen years of digging, pumping and spending, Standedge Tunnel was open and the Huddersfield Canal complete. 133 years later it was abandoned. Tunnel End near Marsden, nine miles south-east of Huddersfield on the Oldham road (A62), is the northern end of Standedge Tunnel, the longest canal tunnel in Britain and perhaps the greatest monument to late eighteenth century canal mania.

The Huddersfield to Ashton-under-Lyne narrow-boat canal was intended to be the vital link in the first and shortest trans-Pennine route between Manchester and Hull. At Huddersfield it would meet Ramsden's Canal, which took boats into the Calder & Hebble system, while at Ashton it would eventually be able to join the Ashton Canal for Manchester, under construction in 1794 when the Huddersfield Canal was initiated. Its backers, many from the Ashton Canal company and looking to increase tolls, ignored the possible difficulties of the route through Standedge and the probable competition from other and easier routes, notably the Rochdale Canal.

Canal mania - the feeling that any canal would be an economic success - was at its height in the late eighteenth century. The canals of the 1760s-70s - which were major links built when finance was readily available - had generally proved lucrative, but from the 1780s the urge to build a canal, any canal, produced the best network in Europe and not a few ruined speculators.

The Huddersfield Canal has seventy-four locks as well as the tunnel, and was an engineering nightmare almost from the start. Tunnelling began at both ends of the 3 mile 176 yard stretch under Standedge, with several

The first (right, opened 1849) and second (opened 1871) Standedge railway tunnels at Tunnel End, near Marsden.

vertical shafts sunk from above to assist with water pumping. After five years of construction, parts of the canal were open and a little over a mile of tunnel driven; much money was owed by the company shareholders, some of whom were bankrupt, had left the country or died. Work continued, although a section of aqueduct near Ashton was carried away by floods and occasionally the men could not be paid in full. In 1800 a mining engineer was brought in to advise on the tunnel, and by 1804 the company were beginning to consider, rather late in the day, how the tunnel was to be worked. With no towpath, boats would have to be 'legged' through, in other words pushed along by pressure of foot against

An aqueduct takes the River Colne over the present railway line (opened in 1894) and canal at Tunnel End.

tunnel wall or roof. Although the company recommended building a towpath through the tunnel, the shareholders would not meet the extra expense.

The two ends of the tunnel met in June 1809, but the catalogue of disasters continued with the failure of the company's bankers in September 1810, and two months later a reservoir burst at Diggle which cost five lives. The Huddersfield Canal finally opened six and a half years after the Rochdale Canal, cost a little over £400,000 and was never a great commercial success.

The tunnel, Britain's most expensive as well as longest, was nine feet wide, stood nine feet above the waterline and had three internal

Looking towards Marsden from the Huddersfield Canal at Tunnel End, where the narrow canal emerges from the Pennines.

passing places (although entry at either end was restricted to particular time periods). Legging a laden boat through the tunnel took three and a half hours.

The canal tunnel is one of four tunnels following the same route under Standedge from Tunnel End. The first railway tunnel, on the London & North Western Railway's Sheffield-Manchester line, opened in 1849. Canal traffic dwindled as further tunnels were bored: a second single-track tunnel in 1871 was followed by a double-track tunnel in 1894. Interconnecting shafts linked rail and canal tunnels, and railway engineers used the canal tunnel for carrying building materials.

The Leeds-Manchester line still uses the 1894 Standedge railway tunnel, the journey between Marsden and Greenfield, a mile from the Lancashire border, taking only nine minutes. Standing before the pair of disused railway tunnels is a daunting experience; chill Pennine air emanates from the blackness, and one half-expects a phantom locomotive to thunder along the grassy line into the cavern beyond.

At the start of the eastward descent from Saddleworth Moor into the Holme Valley on the A635, an exposed moorland side-road heads north, leaving the Peak District National Park just before Meltham and Meltham Mills. Here we find a miniature version of Saltaire, a model village built in the 1840s-60s by millowner James Brook for his workers.

William Brook established a woollen mill near Meltham in the late eighteenth century; it was converted to cotton spinning by 1805 and became one of the largest cotton mills in Yorkshire, with six separate mill buildings erected before 1850 (now mainly demolished).

The village development includes Tudor terraced houses, a church and schools, all set beside a landscaped valley called the People's Pleasure Grounds. The Pleasure Grounds were laid out by renowned Leeds landscape gardener Joshua Major. James Brook lived nearby in a Greek Revival mansion.

Wilshaw, a mile along the A6107 towards Holmfirth, was created by millowner Joseph Hirst in similar philanthropic vein between the 1850s and his death in 1874. He built an unusual Romanesque church in 1862-3, and added Italianate almshouses in 1870-1 for retired employees, following this by a school and an open quadrangle of terraced houses. The village is one of the best works of architects John Kirk & Sons of Huddersfield and Dewsbury.

Two miles east of Wilshaw in the valley of the River Holme is Holmfirth, now a television star in its own right and a genuinely picturesque village. Its steep hills and cobbled streets are crammed into two valleys; there is a large church, a Classical town hall, an ornate Methodist chapel and an early purpose-built cinema (the Valley, 1912) but individual buildings are less important in Holmfirth than the setting, which provides constantly changing views.

To the south of the village, the now-disused route of the Sheffield-Manchester railway followed the south bank of the River Don from Penistone, until going underground at Dunford Bridge, three miles south of the B6106.

The headwaters of the Don at Dunford Bridge are now diverted into spectacular reservoirs, and the castellated portals of the Woodhead Tunnel, which took the railway into Derbyshire, are still visible. The first tunnel, a 3 mile 22 yard single track bore with an almost elliptical arch, was opened in 1845. Construction took six years, and although the navvies were well paid their living conditions were appalling, simply rough stone huts out on the moors. They were paid only once every nine weeks to reduce the risk of drunkenness.

A second single-track tunnel opened in 1852 and a double-line tunnel 102 years later. Work on the 1954 tunnel resulted in six fatal accidents, compared with twenty-six killed in building the earliest tunnel and twenty-eight perishing in a cholera epidemic during construction of the second. The 1954 bore at Woodhead was the third longest railway tunnel in Britain; all three tunnels are now closed.

The village of Penistone existed before the Norman Conquest, and remained a small settlement until the growth of the cloth trade, when it was transformed into a centre for cottage industry. Its role as a market town expanded in the eighteenth century, but the arrival in the nineteenth century of the steel industry from Sheffield, in the form of Cammell Laird & Company, changed the nature of Penistone completely.

The steelworks spawned a model village, Cubley Garden Village, to the south of the town in 1921-2. The architect Sir Herbert Baker produced gabled cottages of concrete blocks which convincingly pass for stone. It was an odd commission for Baker, who had worked on New Delhi with Lutyens and normally designed large institutional buildings in the south of England.

Sheffield is only fifteen miles distant, but the indirect approach is more fun and much more scenic, south along the Pennine edge for a grand view over the city. Leave Penistone heading south to Cubley, but turn right at the Green to Hartcliff Hill, recognisable by the tower near its top. This plain, round tower was built about 1851 by a local mason, but as to why, we do not know.

On the hilltop go left and then right shortly after, down to Underbank Reservoir and Midhopestones, where the tiny church, built in 1705, has box pews and a Jacobean pulpit. Follow the road straight through the village and up to Ewden Height, where it begins to bend steeply down to the woods ringing Ewden Beck.

Cross the beck and climb again, past the earthworks - possibly Iron Age - on the lower slopes of Broomhead Moor. This long entrenchment was part of the defences of the Bradfield area to the south-east. The Broomhead Hall estate lies below the road overlooking the beck. The hall itself, built in 1831 using the Tudor style, was demolished around 1978, although the stables still survive.

The left turning to the south of the estate leads the explorer down to the enticingly-named Wigtwizzle, and a mile further south are more Iron Age defensive works, Bar Dyke, a ditch and rampart running north-east for a quarter mile from the road where it begins to descend into the valley. A left turn at the next junction will bring you to High and Low Bradfield, picturesque villages hanging on to the hillside above the River Loxley. There is a motte and bailey castle and a fine, large Perpendicular church, St Nicholas.

From Bar Dyke, press on for another four miles - bearing right at all junctions - to Strines, where a magnificent view awaits. Directly east is Bradfield Moor, between the valleys and reservoirs of Don tributaries the Loxley and Rivelin, and the edge of Sheffield is six miles distant. Steep and craggy Derwent Edge, two miles to the west, forms the Yorkshire border with Derbyshire and is the watershed between Derwent and Don river systems.

Below Strines to the east are the Strines and Dale Dyke reservoirs, which can be reached by several lanes leading off the Strines road or from Bradfield by following the road running west, parallel to the river; the bulk of the eighty foot high Dale Dyke dam dominates the view. But this is not the original dam. The first Dale Dyke dam was built between 1859 and 1864, to close the valley for one of a series of reservoirs constructed from the 1850s by the Sheffield Waterworks Company to serve the increasing needs of industry.

Mid-nineteenth century Sheffield suffered severe water shortages, and the water which did find its way into the city was often polluted, as upstream cottage industry used the streams for power and to carry away waste. All along the Loxley at that time were small-scale water-powered cornmills, knife-grinding works and wire mills, an idyllic vision in beautiful countryside which hid the realities of work, particularly silicosis generated from dust taken in by grinders working in unventilated conditions.

Techniques of earth-fill dam construction had changed little over the previous century, and basically involved building up an earth and rock embankment on either side of a central core consisting of puddled clay, a mixture of clay, sand and water which becomes impervious to water. Work began on the Dale Dyke dam on New Year's Day

1859, under the superintendence of John Gunson, resident engineer of the Waterworks Company, with John Towlerton Leather as consulting engineer. Leather had been the company's chief engineer between 1830 and the early 1840s, when he began a lucrative career as a contractor; he spent little time at the Dale Dyke works.

Construction of the dam had been estimated to take two years, but hidden springs caused difficulties with the impermeable core; at last, by Friday the 11th March 1864 the ninety-five feet high wall was almost complete. Behind the 418 feet length of embankment stretched almost a mile of water reaching 100 feet in depth; over 700 million gallons of water were held back by the dam.

On that Friday a gale blew from the west, causing waves on the surface of the water and ripples of discontent amongst the engineers and navvies. Gunson checked the structure during the afternoon, but it was not until early evening that a workman found a crack in the outer embankment. Later that night Gunson returned to the dam and attempted to ease the water pressure by opening the valves of the outlet pipes, but the storm brought rain and blew water over the top of the embankment.

Still there appeared no real danger, as the crack looked superficial, but suddenly a torrent came over the embankment and the dam was breached; a triangular hole 300 feet across at its top and 80 feet deep was gouged out by the water, which rushed in a mighty wave down the Loxley Valley towards Sheffield. It took about three minutes for the 'Great Flood' to reach Bradfield. By then the wave was travelling at nearly thirty feet a second, tossing boulders in the air as it went. The wall of water in the narrow valley was fifty feet high. Cottages and mills were demolished as the flood ploughed on into Sheffield, causing havoc at homes and in steelworks, and finally settling in the Attercliffe area. The Great Flood took the lives of almost 250, destroyed 800 houses and flooded another 4,357.

The immediate aftermath of the disaster was mud, shortly followed by tourists, wading around in the mud in Sheffield and picking over the remains of the dam up in the valley. What lay behind the collapse? Engineers at the time could not agree, but a modern verdict suggests poor positioning of pipes in the puddle clay. This allowed water seeping through the dam to erode it internally, causing the centre to subside. Whatever the reason, the collapse was a landmark in construction history, persuading engineers to move from earth-fill to masonry dams.

Sheffield, of course, was now in a far worse position as regards its water supply, and after much discussion the reservoir programme was resumed. The Agden Reservoir, north of Bradfield, was completed in 1869, the Strines in 1871 and the new and smaller Dale Dyke dam in 1875. East of Bradfield the largest reservoir of the Loxley series, the Damflask, was built by the late 1870s but was only in full use from 1896 because of seepage problems. In the peaceful countryside alongside the reservoirs now, it is hard to imagine the horrific wall of water crashing down to Sheffield on that March night in 1864.

Rather than taking the most direct route into Sheffield from Strines, a diversion north through Bradfield will take the traveller across the Don at Oughtibridge and up Jaw Bone Hill, giving a good view back over the city from the Birley Stone.

Two miles further through Grenoside is Ecclesfield, with its large Perpendicular parish church, St Mary, situated on the northern edge of the town. It has a fine and varied display of nineteenth century stained glass, but is best remembered for Alfred Gatty, vicar of St Mary for sixty-three years until the age of ninety. His wife and daughter set up what was almost a cottage industry producing children's books and magazines. Mrs Margaret Gatty edited *Aunt Judy's Magazine*, which was published during 1866-85 and attracted writers of the calibre of Lewis Carroll and Hans Christian Andersen. Their daughter, Juliana Horatia Ewing (1841-85), contributed stories and published books, beginning with *Melchior's Dream* in 1862. Juliana, nicknamed Aunt Judy when young, was one of ten children and thus well-qualified to write about family battles, although she also specialised in sickly deathbed scenes.

Not far away on Wordsworth Avenue (along High Street from St Mary and right after half a mile) is a rather different church, St Paul, designed by Basil Spence & Partners in 1958-9. Its walls zig-zag slightly, reminiscent of Spence's Coventry Cathedral, and there is a detached campanile, but it is less than uplifting. Many unprepossessing buildings were erected in the 1950s and 1960s, but the churches and working men's clubs of that era are prizewinners for consistency of dismal design.

Cross the motorway and head six miles east to Rotherham, a town that is often over-shadowed by neighbouring Sheffield.

Rotherham's image is that of a decaying steel town, but reality, especially when the sun shines through the trees in All Saints Square, is more complex.

In medieval times Rotherham's cattle market, established in 1316, was one of the most important in the region. The happy position of the town, between the agricultural producers of Lincolnshire and Nottingham-shire and the urban consumers of Lancashire, ensured prosperity until the late nineteenth century, by which time heavy industry was thriving. Although modern Rotherham has lost many of its iron, steel and other industrial works - even the steelworks which was once a blazing landmark beside the York to Sheffield railway line - there are still several major steelworks in production.

Rotherham's finest building is All Saints Church. The tower, its earliest remaining element, was begun in 1409 but Anglo-Saxon and Norman churches stood on the same site. The present church is mainly fifteenth century (but restored by George Gilbert Scott in 1873-5); its 180 foot spire is the town's outstanding motif. Inside the stately sandstone church are an octagonal pulpit dating from 1604, good carved choir stalls and stained glass by the prolific Victorian producers Clayton & Bell and Heaton, Butler & Bayne.

Just south of the church was the old centre of Rotherham, based around High Street and the Crofts, once the site of the cattle market. Imperial Buildings on the High Street was built in 1907 using the Jacobean Revival style; its red-brick façade is topped by an excess of chimney stacks. It comprised offices above shops with an internal shopping arcade; many shops have retained good original shopfronts and the arcade is centred on a jolly wooden kiosk.

By walking north of the church along Bridgegate and left over Chantry Bridge the visitor will find another medieval remnant, the Bridge Chapel of our Lady. The chapel was begun about 1482 and has two storeys, battlements and pinnacles, but is quite plain and much restored.

Also in 1482 the College of Jesus was founded at All Saints by Archbishop Thomas Rotherham of York. Its presence ensured that the town became an academic centre, but the Dissolution saw the end of the college, and perhaps indirectly the beginning of modern Rotherham.

The first ironworks was established at Rotherham by Samuel Walker, who was originally a schoolmaster, and who was still teaching around 1741 when he built his first furnace in a nail-making shop at Grenoside. It proved so successful that he gave up teaching and became a full-time ironmaster, building an ironworks west of Rotherham at Mas-brough in 1746.

The site was close to the River Don, which provided transportation and water power, although from 1760 the latter was the source of a long-drawn-out argument between Walker and the Don Navigation Company. Both parties viewed with suspicion the other's calls on the limited water supply; in September 1770, Walker delayed traffic on the navigation by running his rolling mill at Thrybergh, north-east of Rotherham, even on Sundays.

Walker's works expanded west to Holmes and, after the ironmaster's death in 1783, moved east into Rotherham itself in 1792, but the company closed down in the early 1820s.

Walker was interred in a mausoleum in the graveyard of the Independent chapel in College Road (a continuation west of Chantry Bridge). The chapel, which contains many memorials to the Walker family, is currently a warehouse. Walker, a Nonconformist like many ironmasters, built the chapel himself.

Samuel Walker's son Joshua Walker hired John Carr to design his Rotherham town house, Clifton House, in 1783; it is now the town museum and stands on the edge of Clifton Park, east of the town centre. It is a pleasant sandstone Classical pile of five bays, with a pediment and central Venetian window. The well-preserved interior decorative scheme was carried out by John Platt around 1784, and includes a cantilevered marble stair, now with cast iron supports.

The Platts were Rotherham's leading mason-architects in the eighteenth century. John Platt, who took charge of the family firm when still a teenager, expanded the business to include marble-working and ceramics. He helped found the Rotherham Pottery in 1765, eventually selling out to Samuel Walker seven years later. Platt worked as a mason at Wentworth Castle and Wentworth Woodhouse, and designed country houses in the Rotherham area, but his numerous sons tended towards the armed forces rather than architecture, and none continued the family business.

Rotherham's redevelopment has been less publicised than nearby Sheffield's dramatic shopping and sporting endeavours, and for those who thrive on the harsh realities of twentieth century industrial economics, the four mile canalside walk from west of Rotherham to the centre of Sheffield provides pointed illustrations of the Industrial Revolution and its aftermath.

Begin at Tinsley, midway between Sheffield and Rotherham. Here, at Wharf Road, the Don Navigation to the west met the Sheffield & Tinsley Canal running east. The Sheffield Canal was built in 1816-19 at a cost of £104,719, raised by shares and borrowing. It was an expensive venture, as land costs were high and the route chosen was to the south of the Don, necessitating twelve locks (now eleven). Coal-carrying ensured that it was fairly profitable, however, and it remains open.

The view west from the canal at Tinsley is more brutal than picturesque, with trucks on the staggering motorway viaduct (built in 1967) thundering close by. Beyond the tiers of traffic is Sheffield, the green dome of its shopping wonderland Meadowhall to the right. Contrasts between the grubby remnants of old industries and brightly-packaged new structures rapidly become apparent along the towpath.

The city of Sheffield has a wonderful site. It is centred on the meeting point of a southerly bend of the Don with the little River Sheaf which runs to the south-west. Hills nestle in the Don's loop and either side of the Sheaf, giving the city constantly changing levels. Pennine moorland is never far from the centre on the west.

An Iron Age fort existed to the north of the Don on Wincobank Hill, and was followed by an Anglian settlement. In the early twelfth century William de Lovetot, lord of Sheffield, built a castle just south-west of the meeting of Sheaf and Don, defending its western flank with a moat. A village grew up to the west of the castle, along what is now High Street, with a market and church nearby. De Lovetot encouraged coal and iron working, which together with agriculture helped the community into a more prosperous state.

Although water-powered mills had been established as early as the twelfth century in Sheffield, it was not until the end of the fourteenth century that the potential of its streams and rivers for providing power was more fully realised. By that time the metalworking trades had made great advances, and before the end of the sixteenth century Sheffield's cutlery had acquired an international reputation.

As the number of grinding wheels increased, dams were made to control the water flow, each feeding a goit or mill race. When the use of water power was at its height during the seventeenth and eighteenth centuries there were over 160 water-powered mills in Sheffield, many of which continued in use well into the nineteenth century.

Sheffield was a nationally important centre for the production of cutlery and sharp-edged agricultural tools by the start of the eighteenth century, but in the 1740s two inventions occurred which led to diversification of the industrial base: Thomas Boulsover introuced a method of silver-plating copper sheet; and Benjamin Huntsman discovered a means of producing cast steel.

Boulsover's mill was at Whiteley Wood, on the western outskirts of Sheffield, and was powered by Porter Brook which flows into the city along Sharrow Vale. Around 1742 Boulsover managed to melt silver and fuse it with a copper alloy in such a form that the metals could be rolled out together, producing a plate which looked like silver but was much cheaper. It became known as Old Sheffield Plate, and production flourished for a century until the invention of electroplating.

Huntsman was a clockmaker who experimented with steel-making in order to produce a metal suitable for clock springs. He lived at Handsworth, just east of Sheffield, where he found a heat-resistant clay that proved the key to his new process, which involved heating iron to a high temperature in a crucible for five hours.

Eventually, in the early 1740s, he produced a very hard steel, which was initially unpopular with local cutlers as it was difficult to work. However, French cutlers were quick to buy the new product and Huntsman soon built a works at Attercliffe, which began the long association of Sheffield and steel-making.

For Sheffield, dependent on trade for its livelihood, communication with the world beyond the Pennines was always vitally important. The Sheffield Canal in 1819 was followed by a branch railway line through Rotherham to connect with the main London line in 1838, but the cutlers in particular wanted direct connections with Manchester and London; topography was the problem, with hills to the south and west. However, the western route through Woodhead Tunnel was opened up in 1845 and the London route in 1870.

In eighteenth century Sheffield, industry was located around the old town centre and along the valley floors, where cutlers had both their homes and workshops. At the end of the nineteenth century, many prosperous industrialists had moved away from the centre, building mansions on the hills to the west. By 1888 the population of Sheffield was about 300,000 and it was awarded city status in 1893.

The combination of movement from the centre, building in suburban parklands and de-industrialisation has left Sheffield today with a nucleus of attractive Victorian buildings, a number of elegant mansions now used by institutions and set in green surroundings away from the centre, and an exciting collection of modern structures rising from previously industrial sites near the Don.

But back to the canal: from Wharf Road at Tinsley, hurry along the towpath under the motorway towards the jolly green roofline of Meadowhall, opened in 1990 on the site of a disused steelworks and offering 1.2 million square feet of shopping experience to the people of Sheffield, not to mention the other nine million or so who live within an hour's journey. Architects Chapman Taylor Partners have designed the outer container to appear as a fortified town, with high walls, turrets and even a moat (which acts as the service road). From afar - and the motorway gives as good a view as any - the effect is mildly ludicrous, although the dome would look perfect on a seafront. But go inside and it is, of course, a different and very popular world. The design highlight is the Oasis, a circular food-court with an anglicised Mediterranean theme dominated by a wall of video screens. A Spanish holiday with incessant television might be hell for some; back to the towpath and reality.

Stroll on a mile, climbing gently beside the complex of locks and pools which allowed canal boats to descend from the Sheffield basin to the Don, and pass under Broughton Lane. The huge box of the Don Valley Arena

The Don Valley Stadium, from the Sheffield Canal.

appears on the north bank, followed within half a mile by the yellow ladders and white sails of the Don Valley Stadium. The arena (for indoor sports) and the stadium were built by Sheffield City Council to house the World Student Games of 1991; a sporting success, though overlooked by southern-based media, but an economic failure.

The Terminal Warehouse and Grain Warehouse, from under the Straddle Warehouse in Sheffield's Canal Basin.

The legacy of the games is an unparalleled set of sports facilities of high architectural quality. The stadium, designed by the city council's Department of Design and Building Works, cost £30 million and - like the arena - took the place of a steelworks. The exciting and fashionable tent-style stadium grandstand roof is already a landmark in the Don Valley. The roof, supported by the bright yellow ladder-masts, is actually Teflon-coated glassfibre; the result is a light and airy grandstand with unobstructed viewing.

The canal basin is around a mile and a half away, a robust stroll in which the walker

The Nicholson family memorial in Sheffield General Cemetery.

passes close to nineteenth century wharves, warehouses and works. These are not always pretty. The canal itself is well-used by anglers and amblers, and the hum of machinery penetrates the walls of buildings a century or more past their prime, a sound which is still very evocative.

The Cadman Street crossing, near the city centre, is made by an oblique bridge, probably dating from 1819. Then comes the massive Wicker Viaduct, which takes the railway across roads, river and canal. It was built in 1848-9 for the Manchester, Sheffield & Lincolnshire Railway, and is seen at its most grandiose where it bridges the Wicker (a main road), a quarter mile west of the canal. The Sheaf Works on Maltravers Street is soon visible to the right, with a restrained Classical frontage. The works was built in 1822-6 to manufacture steel and cutlery, and is the earliest surviving steelworks of its size in the city.

On to the canal basin (entry from Wharf Street or via the towpath), which presents the walker with a little-changed prospect of a nineteenth century working wharf. At the far end of the basin is the Terminal Warehouse, built when the canal was constructed. An arched opening to the basin gave access for boats. To its north is the Grain Warehouse, dating from the late nineteenth century. The Straddle Warehouse (1895) has an open ground floor, which enabled boats to load and unload direct from the canal. Such is the sense of enclosure that it is not difficult to imagine the basin in full industrial swing.

Now for the city centre, the world beyond the walls of the canal basin. Head diagonally across the huge roundabout to the south of the basin (there are walkways) for a modern antidote to industry. Here the Ponds Forge International Sports Centre, on yet another old steelworks site, presses its immaculate grey and white bulk into the streetscape. Inside the eye-catching curve of its glass wall is a leisure pool, but the rationale for this World Student Games building was the

*The Ponds Forge
International Sports
Centre.*

The Ponds Forge Sports Centre.

creation of an international-standard swimming and diving facility, whose pools are contained by the cavernous vault on the south side. Architects of the £53 million complex were FaulknerBrowns.

Glance up eastwards as you leave Ponds Forge, to where the vast Park Hill and Hyde Park Estate flat complexes once overlooked the Sheaf Valley and the city centre.

Park Hill, designed in 1956-61 by city architect J L Womersley, housed 3,500 in long blocks of flats arranged on a polygonal plan, which was laid out to make the most of the views over Sheffield. The Hyde Park Estate,

Sheffield Town Hall.

One of the three conservatories in Sheffield Botanical Gardens.

begun in 1962, rose beyond Park Hill and housed 4,600 in towers and huge, long blocks of flats. The flats were deck access, in which bridges between blocks formed roads in the sky; it was a most attractive architectural concept, but one which eventually failed in the face of real-life behaviour, and all tenants were moved out by 1989. The flats accom-modated participants in the World Student Games, and will be partly demolished and partly refurbished during the early 1990s. Thus only the smaller blocks survive from Womersley's grand landscaped vision of Sheffield.

Sheffield's civic buildings are clustered together west of Ponds Forge across Arundel

Gate, a divisive dual carriageway. Turn right from Ponds Forge and right again along Pond Hill, bearing left at Pond Street and using a subway to emerge into Tudor Square, between the Lyceum and Crucible Theatres. The square is overlooked by the domineering red-brick tower of Victoria Hall, a Methodist church built in 1908. The Crucible is housed in an elongated red and white box which, given the theatre's position in the snooker world, aptly resembles a sports centre.

The Lyceum Theatre also features a red and white colour scheme but its 1897 façade is more frothy dessert than the Crucible's bread and jam. It is the work of W G R Sprague but was refurbished, with an extension behind the proscenium arch, in 1991 after a long period when the future of the theatre was in doubt.

Oddly, the unashamedly modern extension now appears more original than the Sprague section of the façade, perhaps a result of suspicions induced by a surfeit of post-modern pastiche architecture, but the interior is delightful; Rococo plasterwork covers every available surface. Sprague, the son of an actress, was a particularly elegant architect who produced forty theatres between 1890 and 1916. The Lyceum is his only remaining work outside London, where he was responsible for Wyndhams and the Albery, amongst many others.

Past the Crucible and left along Norfolk Street to the town hall and its extensions, a dominating group in a city centre generally lacking in high-quality buildings.

The sandstone town hall was erected in 1890-7 and designed by London architect Edward Mountford, who won the commission in competition. His style developed into a hefty Edwardian Baroque, exemplified by his Old Bailey. The town hall, its 193 foot tower topped by a statue of Vulcan, Roman god of fire and metalworking, is a decent though unexciting building now lacking a helpful setting.

By 1901 the council needed more space, and extensions were built in 1910 and 1919-23; in the late 1970s a set of basically hexagonal offices across Norfolk Street were added. In style, the most recent extension is modern and functional, and has a façade with the appearance of badly crumpled packaging.

Sheffield's happy topographical situation and plethora of parks ensures optimum views over the city for those escaping from the centre. Out at Weston Park, a mile west of the centre along the A57, is the Mappin Art Gallery, an elegant Classical building of 1886-8 fronted by a colonnade of giant Ionic columns. The architects, Thomas Flockton and E M Gibbs, were local and the style monumental.

Monuments galore can be found at the General Cemetery in its picturesque setting above Porter Brook. (Take the A625 Ecclesall Road west from the centre, then look for Cemetery Avenue on the left at the Sharrow Vale shops.) The Nonconformist cemetery was opened in 1836 by the General Cemetery Company, with buildings and layout by Sheffield architect Samuel Worth. He designed a splendid Doric gateway and chapel, as well as the company's offices, all set amongst trees and rampant greenery. Along an eerie path near the brook, over 250 catacombs tunnel into the hillside. An Anglican extension to the cemetery opened in 1848 with its own spired and church-like chapel by William Flockton and his son Thomas.

Almost directly across Ecclesall Road from the cemetery (up Thompson Road) are the Botanical Gardens, with a group of three elegant but dilapidated conservatories dating from 1837-8.

In the steeply sloping grounds of the Rivelin Glen Cemetery is one of the most interesting buildings in Sheffield, a chapel whose interior displays some of the best of late nineteenth century decorative arts skills. (Take the A61, then A6101 west of the centre; the cemetery is on the left shortly after the road bends left at Malin Bridge.)

The Catholic cemetery opened in 1862 but the chapel, built in 1877-8, was given by a Quaker couple, the Fosters, to commemorate Catholic priest Father Fitzgerald's work with the city's slum dwellers. The Fosters spent £2,000, much of which must have been accounted for by the superlative interior, in which Nathaniel Westlake had a strong hand. There is colourful stained glass and painted decoration, as well as sculpture and a series of terracotta panels showing the stations of the cross.

High in the south-eastern corner of Meersbrook Park (two miles south of the city, just off the A61) is the Bishops' House, a timber-framed house built around 1500. Traditionally, the brothers John and Geoffrey Blythe, bishops of Salisbury (1494-9) and Lichfield and Coventry (1503-33) respectively, were said to have occupied the house, but there is no proof for this suggestion. Its interior shows alterations made between 1500 and 1700 as the owners, probably one of the minor gentry or yeoman farmers, became more

The Doric chapel in Sheffield General Cemetery.

prosperous. A mile south of Meersbrook Park, leave the A61 for Abbey Lane (B6068), to find the remains of Beauchief Abbey, a Premonstratensian foundation dating from 1183. The Premonstratensians were a fairly puritanical order, and proved less than successful in England. At Beauchief, a pretty site above the

Sheaf, the canons mined coal, farmed sheep and built a church, of which the west wall is the only remnant. The little church of St Thomas à Becket was built onto this wall about 1660, and still has its original furnishings including box and family pews.

Just west of the abbey, along Abbey Lane and left on to the A621 Abbeydale Road, is the Abbeydale Industrial Hamlet, now a charming and even picturesque vision of Sheffield industry but at its peak a cauldron of intense activity. The millpond, easily seen from the southbound train, is a calm contrast to the busy works which has been a museum since 1970.

The site on the Sheaf may have been in industrial use as early as 1685, but expansion followed the enlargement of the millpond dam in 1777; a tilt forge, with water-powered hammers, was built in 1785 and a crucible steel furnace was on site by the 1830s. The main product was scythes. The Abbeydale works closed in 1933, although the crucible was in use during the Second World War. The hamlet today retains its structure of small, stone-built cottages complete with machinery, including four water wheels; only the smoke and noise is missing.

Half a mile after passing the industrial hamlet, the railway from Sheffield enters Dore Station. The Dore line connects Sheffield with both Manchester and London, via a pair of tunnels just south of the station. To the east is Bradway Tunnel, which goes underground for just over a mile at nearby Bradway Bank. It was the vital link in the long-awaited Sheffield-London line and opened in 1870. It leads to Chesterfield through a ridge composed of hard rock and shale, which made construction difficult, and in addition the engineers had to deal with numerous springs. Today's Sheffield Station was built for this line, and stands upon arches crossing the Sheaf.

Totley Tunnel, at over three and a half miles long the second longest railway tunnel in Britain, was another engineering triumph. It begins to burrow under the Pennines towards Manchester at Hillfoot, a mile and a half from Dore Station. It was built in 1884-93 by the Midland Railway to compete with other trans-Pennine routes through the Woodhead and Standedge tunnels, and is still in use today, taking the traveller from Dore swiftly into the byways of Derbyshire.

But let us not end this grand tour of the West Riding staring into a tunnel, no matter how brilliant a piece of engineering it may be.

Head north from Hillfoot across Hathersage Road (A625) to Ringinglow village at the foot of the moors, where an octagonal Gothick toll-house, built around 1795, may be found. Here drivers may follow the moorland road towards Hathersage, bearing left past Higher Tor for dramatic views back over Sheffield from Hathersage Moor.

Better still, walkers may take a byway, which follows the route of a turnpike road leading south-west from Ringinglow over Burbage Moor; after a mile and a half it is crossed by a footpath running west, down into the valley of Burbage Brook and up to a wonderful panoramic viewpoint at the site of an ancient fort, Carl Wark.

From the fort, a path leads west to the very end of the Riding - the Derbyshire border, which runs along the A625 from near Millstone Edge. About a mile and a half east of Millstone

Edge on the A625 stands an inn with fine mullioned and transomed windows; this is the Fox House Inn.

Here the traveller may contemplate the sheer size of the West Riding, the amazing complexity of its history, the skill of its engineers and architects, and the enduring power of its landscape. A traveller who has pursued the sights and sites of Yorkshire thus far may also feel it is time to pause for refreshment, as two Ridings more await the explorer.

Glossary of Architectural Terms

apse Semicircular end to a building, normally a chancel or chapel.

arcade Series of arches supported by columns; may be free-standing or attached to a building. Also means a covered way lined with shops.

Art Deco Popular interwar style which took the place of Art Nouveau (*qv*); characterised by geometric forms and bold colour. Its name originated from a 1925 Paris exhibition of decorative arts.

Art Nouveau Style at its height around 1900, which appeared in the mid-1880s and lasted until the first decade of the twentieth century. Its hallmarks were flowing, organic forms and curving lines.

Arts and Crafts Late Victorian movement emphasising craft skills, exemplified by the work of William Morris & Co. Its decorative motifs were often derived from natural objects, while in architecture it featured new uses of vernacular (*qv*) forms.

ashlar Blocks of stone cut with square edges, finished smoothly and laid in even courses.

attached column Column which is not completely free-standing, but linked with a wall to the rear.

bailey Open area of a castle.

ball finial Finial (*qv*) in the shape of a globe.

bargeboard Protective wooden plank attached to the inclined gable (*qv*) ends of a building, often carved decoratively.

Baroque Late seventeenth and early eighteenth century architectural style, using massive, complex, curving forms in bold fashion.

barrel vault Vault (*qv*) with a semicircular cross-section.

battered Wall with an inclined slope.

battlements The alternately raised and lowered upper edge of a parapet wall, often a castle wall.

bay Segment of a building defined by fenestration (*qv*).

beakhead Norman (*qv*) decorative motif resembling a row of bird heads with projecting beaks.

belvedere Summer-house with a view, often sited on a hill in a park; also a viewing tower or turret on top of a house.

bow Curved, and usually mainly glazed, projection from the wall of a building.

box pew Georgian (*qv*) church bench enclosed by high, wooden panels and having a small door.

breastshot Waterwheel in which water is fed onto the wheel at its vertical mid-point; *overshot* indicates that the water arrives at the top of the wheel; while in an *undershot* wheel, the water passes along its lower edge.

Bronze Age British era following the Stone Age and running from around 2100 BC to 700 BC. Marked by the use of bronze for tools, and construction of stone circles.

buttress Brickwork or stonework projecting from a wall and supporting the structure.

canted Oblique corner, often used of bay windows with non-rectangular section.

campanile Bell tower separate from its parent building; also used to describe isolated chimneys.

capital head Uppermost part of a column, often decorated.

castellated Having turrets and battlements (*qv*), as in a castle.

chancel Area forming the east end of a church; the main altar is placed in the chancel, which is reserved for the clergy and choir.

chancel arch Church archway at the west end of the chancel, normally dividing the nave from the chancel.

chantry chapel Chapel endowed to celebrate masses as ordered by its founder.

chapel of ease Chapel built to enable members of a congregation living some distance from the parish church to attend services locally.

chapter house Part of the eastern range (*qv*) of monastic buildings next to the cloister, often circular or polygonal in plan. It was used by the monks for discussion of all types of monastic business.

choir In a church, the section of the chancel where the service is sung.

Classical Various forms of Classical style dominated English architecture from the early seventeenth century until the early nineteenth century. It was originally inspired by Greek and Roman architecture, and then by Renaissance interpretations of past styles. Classical buildings featured traditionally correct proportions and severely restrained decoration.

clerestory Uppermost part of the main walls of a building, with a series of windows; a term often used in church architecture to describe a nave with windows in the upper storey.

colonnade Linked series of columns.

Corinthian Order of Classical (*qv*) architecture involving specified proportions of column and capital, with elaborate foliage decoration of the latter.

Craven Perpendicular Style of Perpendicular (*qv*) church found in Craven area of Yorkshire; churches are normally long and low, with substantial towers.

crenellate Crenellations are also known as battlements; a crenellated wall has alternating higher and lower sections along its upper edge.

crocket Decorative element, often carved in leaf shapes, which appears on Gothic (*qv*) spires, gables (*qv*) and other pre-eminent features.

crossing tower   Church tower sited above the area where nave, chancel and transepts intersect.

curtain wall   Originally it meant the outer wall of a castle, connecting its towers, but is now also applied to any external non-loadbearing wall.

dado   Decorative finish of the lower part (to about waist height) of an internal wall.

Doric   Order of Classical (*qv*) architecture involving specified proportions of column and capital, with very little decoration of the latter.

Edwardian   Building design in the first decade of the twentieth century encompassed a range of styles from severe Classical to highly decorative Edwardian Baroque. These may perhaps all be characterised by a preoccupation with novel interpretations of existing styles, and the search for a new and British architecture. The resulting buildings differed widely in appearance but shared a certain confidence.

Egyptian Revival   The use of motifs, such as obelisks (*qv*) and pyramids, derived from ancient Egyptian architecture. The early nineteenth century and the 1920s are the two most recent revivals, the latter resulting from the discovery in 1922 of the tomb of Tutankhamun.

Elizabethan   Style of the late sixteenth and early seventeenth centuries, typified by symmetrical facades, large, mullioned (*qv*) and transomed (*qv*) windows, and decorative strapwork (*qv*).

encaustic tile   Clay tile of the Victorian period, used mainly as flooring, with decoration originally based on Medieval tile designs. Later Victorian examples featured colourful geometric decoration, and were widely used in public buildings as well as churches.

faience   Inclusive term for all ceramic materials used in an architectural context, such as on a faience façade.

fenestration   The pattern of windows in the wall of a building.

finial   Decorative feature of varying form found on top of spires, gables (*qv*) and other tall architectural elements; originally Gothic (*qv*).

flying buttress   Buttress (*qv*) with lower part detached from the building it supports.

folly   Building with no purpose, at least in terms of normal cost-benefit criteria. Follies are often decorative, with eccentric architectural features, and frequently appear as park ornaments.

gable   The triangular upper part of a wall defined by a pitched roof. Variants include the Dutch gable, which has curved sides and is topped by a pediment (*qv*).

Georgian   Architectural style of the early eighteenth to early nineteenth centuries, with plain, Classical (*qv*) exteriors and more decorative interiors, culminating in those of Robert Adam in the late eighteenth century.

Germano-Gothic   Victorian style in which Gothic (*qv*) is tempered by traditional German elements, particularly turrets, gables and steeply pitched roofs with small dormer windows.

Gothic   **Style** featuring pointed arches, arcading (*qv*) and flying buttresses (*qv*); together they formed a structural system which minimised wall area. It was introduced to Britain in the early twelfth century, becoming known as the Early English style. This developed into the Decorated style, with more prominent decoration and tracery (*qv*), in the latter half of the thirteenth century. By the second half of the fourteenth century the Perpendicular style, with the emphasis on straight, vertical elements, had come to the fore and lasted for around 250 years. The Victorian Gothic Revival was particularly important for church architecture.

Gothick Style of the Gothic (*qv*) Revival of the mid-eighteenth century, which was first applied to pleasure buildings and featured frilly, highly-decorative Gothic motifs.

hammerbeam roof Roof structure formed by a series of roof supports or hammer-posts projecting vertically upward from brackets or hammerbeams set in the top of the wall.

High Victorian Architecture of the mid-nineteenth century, often featuring polychromy (*qv*) and the use of varied building materials.

ice-house Garden outbuilding popular in the eighteenth and nineteenth centuries, often built with country houses; its purpose was to store ice. Frequently built partly underground, and with a roughly egg-shaped internal space.

Ionic Order of Classical (*qv*) architecture involving specified proportions of column and capital, with twin spiral-pattern decoration of the latter.

Iron Age Period from around 700 BC until the time of the Roman invasion; iron was used for tools and weapons.

Italianate Victorian style involving Italian Renaissance elements such as low-pitched roofs, towers and round-headed windows.

Jacobean Style of the early seventeenth century, a development of the Elizabethan (*qv*); important elements were large windows, extravagant decoration and dominant gables (*qv*).

Jacobethan Victorian or Edwardian style combining elements traditionally found in Jacobean (*qv*) and Elizabethan (*qv*) buildings, such as mullioned (*qv*) windows, a high level of decoration and prominent gables (*qv*).

king post Central, vertical timber support–ing a pitched roof, and rising from a beam connecting the tops of the walls to the ridge of the roof.

lancet window Narrow, pointed-arched window.

lychgate Covered gateway at the entrance to a churchyard; originally provided a resting place for coffins.

mansard roof Pitched roof with two differently sloping sections on each side, a steeper section rising from the wall followed by a lower-pitched section reaching the ridge.

Medieval The era between the fifth and fifteenth centuries, from when the Romans left Britain to the coming of the Renaissance. In architectural terms, it encompasses Saxon (*qv*), Norman (*qv*), Romanesque (*qv*) and Gothic (*qv*) periods.

misericord Bracket, often decoratively carved, on the underside of a hinged choir stall or seat; when the stall was raised, the misericord supported the standing chorister.

Moorish Stylistic features used in late Victorian period and taken from ancient Islamic architecture of Spain and North Africa; its main forms are elaborate domes and arcades.

mullion Vertical element separating the sections of a window.

nave   Area forming the west end of a church, which may be extended to the north or south with aisles.

Norman   Architecture of the period from the early eleventh to the mid-twelfth centuries. Its main features are massive structures, round-headed arches and geometrical ornament.

obelisk   Tall, upright column, usually with a square cross-section and tapering towards the top.

oriel   Bay window on an upper floor, unsupported at ground level, thus overhanging.

Palladian   Classical (*qv*) style derived from the buildings of the sixteenth century Italian architect Andrea Palladio, which was introduced to England in the early seventeenth century. The style emphasises symmetry and ancient systems of proportion, and strongly features the colonnade (*qv*), portico (*qv*) and venetian window (*qv*).

pediment   Low-pitched gable (*qv*) above features such as a portico (*qv*), door or window.

Perpendicular   Gothic (*qv*) style dominant between the late fourteenth century and the late sixteenth century, when the Elizabethan (*qv*) style became established. Perpendicular style strongly emphasised vertical architectural elements, as did the more decorative Elizabethan.

Picturesque   Mid-eighteenth to early nineteenth century style, largely used in the context of cottages, country houses and garden design but having broader implications, and partly derived from the images of seventeenth century landscape painting. The style was highly decorative, combining ruggedness with ruins, and used disparate elements such as

Italianate (*qv*) motifs in an asymmetrical fashion. The object was to create a sublime vision by combining nature and architecture.

pilaster   Column projecting only slightly from a wall.

polychromy   Decorated in many colours. Mid-Victorian architects produced polychromy not only by using paint, but by combining different building materials; this technique is known as structural polychromy.

portico   Entrance space of a building, often a house or church, which is covered but normally open to the sides, and has a pediment (*qv*) supported by columns; the whole is in the style of a temple.

prodigy house   Large-scale Elizabethan (*qv*) country house, with huge areas of glazing and abundant decoration.

Queen Anne Revival   The architectural style used for small domestic buildings of the Queen Anne period (early eighteenth century) was revived in the late nineteenth century; in its revival form it emphasised red-brick walls and contrasting white, wooden window frames.

range   A row of buildings.

Regency   Style predominant between the 1790s and the early 1840s; when used strictly, the term relates to the period 1811-20 when the future George IV was prince regent. This neo-Classical style made free use of ancient forms, resulting in eclectic versions of Classical (*qv*) structures, which sometimes verged on the Picturesque (*qv*).

reredos   Screen or similar structure sited behind, and usually above, the altar; often decorated.

Rococo   The final stylistic phase of the Baroque (*qv*), which occurred during the mid-eighteenth century in England, where it was used only for interiors and garden buildings. The elaborately decorative Rococo style emphasised delicacy and lightness of form and colour, as opposed to the sombre heaviness of the Baroque.

Roman   Buildings of the Roman occupation of Britain, which lasted from around AD 43 to AD 409, and included sophisticated baths and temples.

Romanesque   Term used to describe the dominant architectural style of Europe from the tenth century (or before) until the eleventh century, and marked by the use of the round arch; roughly equivalent to the Norman (*qv*) style in Britain. The round-arched Romanesque form also underwent a late Victorian revival.

rood loft   The wooden rood or cross was usually erected at the east end of the nave, on a beam stretching across the upper part of the chancel arch (*qv*). Just below it was the rood loft, a gallery which might itself carry the rood or other images; the loft also stretched across the chancel arch. Rood lofts were introduced in the fifteenth century.

rood screen   Screen beneath the rood loft (*qv*), separating the nave and chancel.

rose window   Large, circular, church window, with tracery (*qv*) pattern radiating from its centre.

rubblestone   Unfinished stone in various shapes, with rough surfaces and few right-angled corners; irregular rubble may be worked into horizontal courses during building, in which case it is known as coursed rubblestone.

rustication   Massive blocks of masonry which are separated by deep, V-shaped joints; often used on the lower part of external walls of large buildings to add weight to the composition.

Saxon   English architecture of the seventh to early eleventh centuries. Simple churches occurred in the seventh century, and towers first appeared in the tenth century; basic geometric decoration was often prominent.

Scottish Baronial   Style originated by architect William Burn around 1830 for Scottish country houses, in which the basic building was adorned with large, circular towers and turrets, often capped by steeply-pitched, conical roofs; the whole was in the Scottish tradition of fortified architecture.

Second Empire   Style current from the 1850s until the end of the nineteenth century; the main elements emphasised the height of the building: turrets, chimneys, domes and the mansard roof (*qv*). The term arises from extensions to the Louvre made by Napoleon III, which used French Renaissance decorative forms.

solar   The upper living-room of a medieval house.

spandrel   Roughly triangular area between the tops of adjacent arches or arched windows; may be decorated.

strapwork   Late sixteenth century decorative motif of intertwined bands.

tie beam   Main horizontal beam in a roof structure, which connects the tops of opposing walls.

timber-framed   Type of building construction in which an open, wooden framework, usually of horizontal and vertical timbers, forms the walls; this frame is then filled in with non-structural matter such as plaster.

tower house   A medieval fortified house, of

three storeys or more in height, most frequently found in Scotland and the north of England.

tracery   Pattern of ribs defining the glazing of the upper section of a window; also used to describe the pattern of decoration on vaults (*qv*).

transom   Horizontal element separating sections of a window.

Tudor   Architecture of the sixteenth century, culminating in the Elizabethan (*qv*) period, when the professional architect came to prominence for the first time.

vault   Arched roof structure, normally in brick or stone, with a semicircular or more complex cross-section; a more complex vault is divided by a pattern of curved ribs.

Venetian window   Window in three vertical sections, of which the central section is taller than the side sections and has a semicircular top.

vermiculated   Type of rustication (*qv*) in which the blocks of masonry are carved with intersecting, curving shapes having the appearance of worm tracks.

vernacular   The architecture of everyday buildings, with the emphasis on the use of locally available materials, as opposed to the style of grander buildings designed by architects.

vestry   Small room, in which the vestments are kept, attached to a church.

Victorian   Architecture of the reign of Queen Victoria (1837-1901), sometimes extended to encompass the reign of William IV (1830-37). A period of stylistic eclecticism in which Gothic (*qv*), Classical (*qv*) and other styles all had their proponents, resulting in the building of varied, and often colourful, structures.

winter garden   Conservatory-style structure, often built of cast iron and glass; popular in the domestic context on a small scale, and as large-scale entertainment buildings (particularly at resorts), from the middle to late nineteenth century.

zigzag   Norman (*qv*) decorative motif of a line turning sharply and alternately to right and left.

Bibliography

The West Riding and its Architecture

M F Barbey, *Civil Engineering Heritage - Northern England* (Thomas Telford 1981).

Gordon Biddle and O S Nock, *The Railway Heritage of Britain* (Michael Joseph 1983).

Chris Brooks, *Mortal Remains* (Wheaton 1989).

Lionel Butler and Chris Given-Wilson, *Medieval Monasteries of Great Britain* (Michael Joseph 1983).

Painton Cowen, *A Guide to Stained Glass in Britain* (Michael Joseph 1985).

Gillian Darley, *Villages of Vision* (Granada 1978).

Colum Giles and Ian H Goodall, *Yorkshire Textile Mills 1770-1930* (HMSO 1992).

Mark Girouard, *The Victorian Country House* (Yale University Press 1979).

Charles Hadfield, *The Canals of Yorkshire and North East England* Vols I and II (David and Charles 1972 and 1973).

Jane Hatcher, *The Industrial Architecture of Yorkshire* (Phillimore 1985).

Gwyn Headley and Wim Meulenkamp, *Follies* (Jonathan Cape 1990).

Phyllis Hembry, *The English Spa 1560-1815* (Athlone Press 1990).

Derek Linstrum, *West Yorkshire Architects and Architecture* (Lund Humphries 1978).

Frank Musgrove, *The North of England: A history from Roman times to the present* (Blackwell 1990).

Nikolaus Pevsner (revised Enid Radcliffe), *Yorkshire: the West Riding* (Penguin 1967).

Ken Powell, *The Fall of Zion* (SAVE Britain's Heritage 1980).

Arthur Raistrick, *West Riding of Yorkshire* (Hodder and Stoughton 1979).

Redundant Churches Fund, *Churches in Retirement, A Gazetteer* (HMSO 1990).

Royal Commission on the Historical Monuments of England, *Rural Houses of West Yorkshire 1400-1830* (HMSO 1986).

Peter F Ryder, *The Medieval Buildings of Yorkshire* (Moorland Publishing 1982).
David Smurthwaite, *Battlefields of Britain* (Webb & Bower 1987).

From Crimple to Crypt
Marcus Binney, 'Axed'(*Landscape* January 1988).
Dan Cruickshank, 'Cullinan's Bold Approach' (*Architects' Journal* 12th August 1992).
Richard Haslam, 'Studley Royal, North Yorkshire' (*Country Life* 27th March 1986).
Malcolm G Neesam, *Exclusively Harrogate* (Smith Settle 1989).
Robert Unwin, *Wetherby* (Wetherby Historical Trust 1987).

Dangerous Corner and the Valley of Desolation
D J H Clifford, *The Diaries of Lady Anne Clifford* (Alan Sutton 1992).
Arthur Gemmell and Colin Speakman, *Dales Way Route Guide* (Stile Publications 1991).

The Midland, the Millionaire and the Manufacturers
Frank Duerden, *Great Walks: Yorkshire Dales* (Ward Lock 1986).
Barbara Hutton and Joyce Martin, *Doorways in the Dales* (North Yorkshire and Cleveland Vernacular Buildings Study Group 1986).
Ian Goldthorpe, *The Ribble Way* (Lancashire County Planning Department 1988).
Miles Hadfield, *A History of British Gardening* (John Murray 1960).
Harry Ree and Caroline Forbes, *The Three Peaks of Yorkshire* (Whittet Books 1988).
Arthur Raistrick, *Malham and Malham Moor* (Dalesman 1947).

Beer, Burmantofts and Brodrick
Janet Douglas and Ken Powell, *St John's Church, Leeds: A History* (Redundant Churches Fund undated).
Janet Douglas, Chris Hammond and Ken Powell, *Leeds: Three Suburban Walks* (Victorian Society 1987).
Janet Douglas and Ken Powell, *Leeds: Three Architectural Walks* (Victorian Society 1982).
Derek Fraser (ed), *A History of Modern Leeds* (Manchester University Press 1980).
Huon Mallalieu, 'Spenfield, Yorkshire' (*Country Life* 24th September 1992).
Ken Powell, 'Leeds' latest' (*Architects' Journal* 25th April 1990).
Temple Newsam (Leeds City Art Galleries 1984).

Worstedopolis
Marcus Binney *et al*, *Satanic Mills* (SAVE Britain's Heritage 1979).
Bradford Metropolitan Council, *Best Listed Buildings in Bradford* (Planning Division, City of Bradford Metropolitan Council 1988).
John Braine, *Room at the Top* (Eyre and Spottiswoode 1957).

James Douet, *Going up in Smoke* (Victorian Society 1991).
Gary Firth, *Victorian Yorkshire at Play* (Hendon Publishing 1989).
Malcolm Hardman, *Ruskin and Bradford* (Manchester University Press 1986).
Cyril Pearce, *The Manningham Mills Strike* (University of Hull 1975).
C Richardson, *A Geography of Bradford* (University of Bradford 1976).

A Skyline of Towers
Calderdale Way Association, *The Calderdale Way* (Metropolitan Borough of Calderdale 1983).
Bernard Jennings *et al*, *Pennine Valley* (Smith Settle 1992)

Into Eastern Extremities
Graham Hudson, *The Aberford Fly Line* (Hudson 1983).
J Douglas Porteous, *Canal Ports: The Urban Achievement of the Canal Age* (Academic Press 1977).
Alan Powers, *Oliver Hill* (Mouton Publications 1989).
Harry Speight, *Lower Wharfedale* (S R Publishers 1969; first published 1902).
Nostell Priory (National Trust 1985).

Defaced to the Uttermost
Marcus Binney, 'Wentworth Woodhouse, Yorks' (*Country Life* 24th January 1991).
Tony Davis, *Wentworth Woodhouse* (Sheffield City Polytechnic 1982).
Jack Simmons, *The Victorian Railway* (Thames and Hudson 1991).
Catherine Slessor, 'Pleasure palace' (*Architects' Journal* 21st March 1990).
R B Wragg, 'The Stand on Hoober Hill' (*Architectural Review* June 1979).

Tunnel and Torrent
Geoffrey Amey, *The Collapse of the Dale Dyke Dam 1864* (Cassell 1974).
B Bunker, *Portrait of Sheffield* (Robert Hale 1972).
Mary Cadogan and Patricia Craig, *You're a Brick, Angela!* (Gollancz 1976).
Colum Giles, *An Architectural Survey of Urban Development Corporation Areas: Sheffield* (RCHME 1989).
Charles Hadfield and Gordon Biddle, *The Canals of North West England* Vols I and II (David and Charles 1970).
C M Ross, *John Platt, Mason-Architect* (Metropolitan Borough of Rotherham 1984).
Catherine Slessor, 'Sporting Revival' (*Architects' Journal* 17th July 1991).
Mary Walton, *Sheffield: Its Story and Achievements* (Sheffield Telegraph 1948).

Index